Disturbed by Mind and Spirit

For the people of St Andrew's, Fulham Fields

Disturbed by Mind and Spirit

Mental Health and Healing in Parish Ministry

Gavin Knight and
Joanna Knight

mowbray

Published by Mowbray, a Continuum imprint
The Tower Building, 11 York Road, London SE1 7NX
80 Maiden Lane, Suite 704, New York NY 10038

www.continuumbooks.com

First published 2009

British Library Cataloguing-in-Publication Data
A catalogue record for this book is available from the British Library.

ISBN 978-0-8264-2775-5

Typeset by Kenneth Burnley, Wirral, Cheshire
Printed and bound by MPG Books Group, United Kingdom

Contents

Foreword

It might seem a far cry from a small and peaceful market town in the Welsh Borders to the London parish which is the scene for the painful drama which lies at the heart of this book. And yet perhaps there is something appropriate in finding that its authors wrote this book out of that setting. For a borderland brings together different things and makes of them something new, and that is exactly what Gavin and Jo are doing here. It is a courageous undertaking, for it has asked of them a willingness to be vulnerable and open, to face up honestly to something which can so easily be denied or hidden or buried. Here we have a priest and a psychologist speaking to us of something which is at once totally specific in an immediate situation, yet at the same time carries a much wider significance. This book comes out of real life, and real love, for it centres on the Eucharist. The connection of liturgy and healing lies at its heart. Theological understanding and psychology become tools working together. The structure of the book means that they are tools placed in the hands of the reader. Here is material that can be used in a variety of different ways. While it can be simply read for its intrinsic interest, it can also be read in order to be studied, and discussed.

What gives this book its particular value is that it is tough and real, and, as a result, searching. This is not some remote, academic, theoretical discussion. It is the work of a husband and wife – an ordained priest and a clinical psychologist – and it comes out of their shared, lived-out and hard-won experience. So we are not allowed to be beguiled by what they have to tell us and then to forget it. We are faced by the question, 'What next? Where do I come in?' It does not matter if the reader is a so-called church official, churchwarden, parish priest, or simply a lay member of the congregation – there are practical implications here about the handling of those stories which, when they are brought out into the light, can tell us so much and deepen our understanding of the way God works through the liturgy to offer healing to a broken world.

Esther de Waal
Christmas Eve, 2008

Acknowledgements

Our thanks to Esther de Waal whose encouragement and editorial input helped motivate and shape the book. Particular thanks also to Dallin Chapman whose many insights and revisions kept us on the straight and narrow; and to Saskia Barnden for all her time, comments and suggestions.

Key people who have influenced us on our journeys, both recent and distant, are: John Austen, Alison Brown, Stuart Burns (OSB), Richard Chapman, Valerie Cryer, Brian Hardy, John Irvine, Emma Joy (SSC), Ralph Pite, Mark Pryce, Laurence Gamlen, Ruth Scott, Brothers Matthew and Paolo of Taizé, Christopher Swift, Joanna Tucker, Richard Woodward and the people of St Alphege with St Catherine. Thanks also to Joe Moffat and Gerry Buckland for some timely reflections; and to Jill and Brian Forsyth for the use of their child-free flat. Thank you to Gavin's parents for their continued support and affirmation. And lastly, to Jo's parents for all their time and support, unfailingly given – without them, this book would not have been written.

Authors' notes

With the exception of St Andrew's, Fulham Fields, and its former incumbent David Paget, all names and identifying information have been changed to protect individuals' identity. In addition, all pastoral and clinical illustrations are representative amalgamations, and do not relate to any one individual in particular.

For ease of reading, 'priest' has been referred to in the masculine pronoun throughout. This in no way reflects the authors' theology – all references are understood to include both men and women.

There is a place within each of our sacred selves that very few would willingly visit, and yet this place is probably more frequented than any other we know. It is a fragile place, fused with the mind and the spirit. It has many terrains, many voices and many magnitudes. So well hidden is this place that, when we find ourselves on its threshold, we turn our gaze from its path and, deep within our unconscious self, a voice is spoken: I am not here, I have not visited this place, tell no one. And so in that moment of buried recognition, we re-frame what we have encountered and seek to sanitize what we have known.

Or do we? Perhaps instead we open the door and risk entering a place from which we might never return; from a place that is so riddled with stigma and myth that, steeped in our society though it is, it only forms the subject of discourse in specialist circles or with a trusted few. It is a sensitive place and it must not be spoken of too loudly. Its limits are poorly defined and its nature unpredictable. Unique to each and every one of us, this place is, we suggest, the landscape of our mental health.

JDK

Introduction

Everyone has mental health needs, whether or not they have a
mental health diagnosis.

(Promoting Mental Health:
A Resource for Spiritual and Pastoral Care, 2004)

Defining mental health

Today's media are constantly reminding us of our fragile mental health.
One by one, it seems, different social groupings fall under the spotlight
as individuals publicly articulate their own experiences of mental health
problems or, in some cases, have them articulated for them. No one
apparently is exempt: our children, our parents, celebrities, sportsmen
and women, politicians, clergy . . . the list is growing, varied and, above
all, inclusive.

In recent years the Church of England has also started to voice a
growing awareness of mental health. In 2004, the Church of England Archbishops' Council published a lengthy document entitled *Promoting Mental
Health: A Resource for Spiritual and Pastoral Care.*[1] It describes mental
health as a continuum 'with people positioned at various points along that
line at different points in their life' (p. 29). *Promoting Mental Health* recognizes, therefore, that the prevalence of mental health problems is high: an
estimated one in six adults experiences mental health problems at any one
time, and one in four adults is likely to experience mental health difficulties in different degrees during the course of one year.

Mental health can be defined as follows:

1

Mental health concerns everyone, and is more than the absence of mental problems. It underpins our health and well-being and influences how we think and feel about ourselves and other people, how we interpret events, and our capacity to learn, communicate and form and sustain relationships. Mental health affects our ability to cope with and manage change, transition and life events such as the birth of a child, redundancy, retirement or bereavement. (*Promoting Mental Health*, 2004, p. 29)

The term 'mental health' encapsulates, therefore, a broad spectrum of psychological difficulties and an all-inclusive spectrum of people. Despite this, the concept of mental health carries with it the potential for misconception, a fear of labelling and stigma. As soon as the term is misunderstood or used idly in any way, the potential for stigma or false assumptions is increased. This is not an excuse for avoiding the terms altogether, but it does highlight the need for mental health to be understood in a broader social context.

Mental health needs in a parish context

To date there is very little literature on the subject of mental health in a parish context. Nonetheless the topic does seem to be finding its way into the vocabulary of parish ministry. *Psychology for Christian Ministry* (Watts, Nye and Savage, 2002), a seminal text, offers a detailed psychological perspective on a wide range of issues in the Church, including two chapters on emotional problems and pastoral counselling; and, more recently, Marion Carson's book, *The Pastoral Care of People with Mental Health Problems* (2008) provides a useful account of a range of mental health difficulties, incorporating suggestions about how ministers might respond to these in pastoral situations.

These books mark the exception, not the rule. And yet, despite the paucity of literature, as a clinical psychologist married to an Anglican priest I have been privy at a personal level to parish priests' increased awareness of mental health issues. The challenge remains how to translate this increased awareness into practice. This need for greater theory–practice links is critical, hence our desire to respond to the times and move a mental health agenda more firmly onto the Anglican map.

*   *   *

For several years Gavin and I have been struck by the enormous pressure that clergy can experience through their call to pastor all people. By virtue of a priest's diverse role, he will inevitably come into contact with a diverse flock, including people with varying degrees of mental instability. The pressure that this can entail was brought into sharp focus when we moved to the West London parish of St Andrew's, Fulham Fields, not least because we were both living and working in the same locality. The differences in the pattern of our days were pronounced. While both working in the so-called 'caring professions', my work as a clinical psychologist was, if you like, 'incognito'. I went to work, I saw clients at work within a given time-frame, I even worked under a separate name and, when I came home, by and large I was able to leave the day's stresses behind. In professional-speak, my boundaries were relatively clear.

For Gavin, by contrast, the boundaries were more tenuous. Pressures often came over the threshold and could be hard to predict. Parish priests have no neat referral system explaining to them the presenting difficulties in advance. In a parish setting, people in need frequently turn up unannounced. While this highlights the wonder as well as the strain of parish ministry, it also reinforces the pressing need to address a significant gap in a priest's training: that is, to raise the awareness and understanding of mental health in a priest's ministry.

This 'gap' has been articulated in the last decade by leaders of Christianity, Islam and Judaism. The aim of 'The Religion and Severe Mental Illness Conference' in April 1999 was 'to raise awareness of the issue of mental illness as the proper concern of religious leaders and those involved in or associated with religion'.[2] At this conference, Chief Rabbi Jonathan Sacks reflected:

> Often clergy are in the front line. They get members of their community approaching them because they have a problem and they need assistance with it. In the majority of cases they haven't the experience or knowledge of what to say or do, or who to recommend the person to.

Jonathan Sacks' comments bring to mind a conversation I had with a friend during his curacy some years ago. James described an incident that had occurred some weeks previously. It was late one evening and the doorbell had rung. When he answered, he was greeted by a man in his forties, not known to him, and clearly distressed. It was difficult to make out what he was saying, for his speech was rapid and incoherent, but James invited him in and spent some time talking to him in his study. The content of this conversation is not important. The very fact of the exchange, however, serves as an example of many such encounters between clergy and parishioners. For James and myself, the incident led to a wider discussion and debate. What, if anything, should he have done? Should he have let him in? Should he have contacted anyone else and, if so, whom? How might he have known, apart from instinct, that the man was suffering from some form of mental illness? How might he struggle with the tension, on the one hand, between parish priest as listener, friend and above all Christ's disciple, and on the other as quasi social worker, health practitioner and stand-in psychologist? These questions do not presume to offer answers. They do, however, highlight the multiple tensions of meeting mental health needs in parish ministry.

*   *   *

In 2002 Gavin and I attended a day's conference on mental health in the Church. The programme for the conference was promising and the ethos of the day focused much attention on the importance of de-stigmatizing mental health. This was both commendable and helpful and is indeed one of our own aims. At the same time I found I sat uncomfortably with some of the discussions. In the effort to 'normalize' mental health, a tendency emerged almost to down-play the potentially devastating and crippling effects of mental health problems on individuals, families, and even communities. This tendency grew out of a genuine desire to achieve empathy for a vulnerable group. Yet out of this effort we somehow managed to distance ourselves from the very people we were seeking to empathize with. It was as though the group's desire for empathy was complicated by an almost contrary impulse: the impulse to sanitize or 'make good' what we had encountered.

In response to this, we tried to describe something of the challenges of our own parish. The parish was diverse in the fullest sense. Bankers, the unemployed, builders, accountants, the homeless, pensioners, single mothers, all gathered there. Not only was there occupational diversity but also great cultural, ethnic and economic difference. The prevalence of mental health needs was high. Complicating, sharpening perhaps, the focus of these needs was the traumatic history of the parish itself. Its previous incumbent, David Paget, had died in 2001 in the vicarage in tragic circumstances. He was believed to have been murdered by a man in his twenties who then killed himself a short while later.

David's murder is one of five murders of priests in the UK since 1996 (Tolson, 2007). Most recently, the tragic death of Paul Bennett, a priest in South Wales, caught the media attention. Paul Bennett was murdered by a man with paranoid schizophrenia and a personality disorder, but who was nonetheless not known to the psychiatric services.[3] These stories serve as tragic and extreme examples of what can and has occurred to priests in parochial ministry. It is hard to refer to the events without inadvertently sensationalizing them, or somehow perpetuating the myth that mental illness and violence are inextricably linked. In fact, mental illness tends to be much less a factor in violence against clergy than other factors such as drug abuse.[4] It would seem, though, that there are two clear consequences that have arisen from these events: first, the need to take clergy safety seriously; and second, the need for the Church to raise its awareness of mental health as an issue. This is true not just for those occasions when mental illness has become associated with high-profile incidents; but, much more typically, for the range of mental health problems that affect each and every one of us in its many shapes and forms.

Aims of the book

This book will seek to explore how issues of mental health in parish ministry can be addressed through the dual perspectives of theology and clinical psychology. These perspectives are informed by two frameworks, liturgical and psychological. Specifically, in the liturgical structure of the Eucharist, there are four movements: Preparation–Gathering, the Liturgy of the Word, the Liturgy of the Sacrament, and the Dismissal. Coincidentally, a clinical psychologist's framework also comprises four key components: assessment, formulation, intervention and evaluation. With almost uncanny ease, each psychological component seems to enjoy a potential for relationship with its liturgical counterpart.

We do not wish to force the relationship between the two disciplines – to impose some psychological model on liturgy which does not really exist. We do, however, wish to draw upon a psychological perspective to help reflect upon the liturgical pattern as a way of deepening our awareness of and response to mental health. Central to this perspective is not *product* (that is, not some textbook understanding of what mental health is and how best to 'treat it') but *process:* that is, how to be alive to it, reflective about it and present with it.

The book is structured as follows: chapters are written in pairs, with each theological chapter followed by its psychological counterpart. Writing alternately, we begin by drawing upon our own personal stories (Chapters 1 and 2) and disciplines (Chapters 3 and 4) in order to put into context our shared perspective of mental health. The remaining chapters (5 to 12) relate to the four liturgical movements and the four key aspects of psychological thinking and practice. All six pairs of chapters conclude with a section entitled 'Integrating Mind and Spirit'. These sections constitute an overview of shared themes and some practical points relating to these themes. The overview is followed by four 'questions' which hopefully can be used as a starting point either for individual reflection or discussion in small groups. Finally, the sections round off with a prayer: our attempt to recognize the sensitivity of the issues at hand and to provide one way of holding these in a safe place. In this way we hope to invite the reader to respond to and debate our shared, albeit tentative understanding of mental health and healing in parish life.

In essence, this book aims to speak to a wide range of people who attend or serve in a parish church and for whom the issue of mental health is relevant. To sum up, our aims are these:

- To provide a training resource to help raise the profile of mental health issues present in parish life.
- To encourage individuals to reflect on their own personal stories, ideas and belief systems and how these might impact on their ministry and/or discipleship in the context of mental health.
- To help recognize and acknowledge that mental health is often a stigmatized, forbidden and misunderstood subject; one which has no clear-cut answers but which challenges our core selves and requires us, if we are to respond to it authentically, to recognize our own strengths and limitations, our areas of expertise and when we need to seek additional help or support.

- To offer hope for the renewal of parish life in general, not necessarily through specific strategies and solutions but through a deepened understanding of our shared stories of brokenness and healing.

This book is not a call for all interested parties, lay or ordained, to 'get psychological', to become somehow experts in mental health and reinvent themselves in a large and complex field which, to clients and professionals alike, is already unwieldy. Rather, it seeks to reflect upon, even celebrate, how theological reflection and psychological thinking might enable individuals to draw upon their unique strengths in the context of parish life and discipleship.

JDK

Part 1

Story-telling

The first two chapters are, above all, about story-telling. They focus on our individual journeys of vocational and professional development from deacon to priest, and assistant psychologist to clinical psychologist. Through this process we seek to explore how our own stories of brokenness and healing are played out in both our personal and our vocational/professional lives. In this way the ground is laid for the book's wider story of brokenness and healing.

This is a narrative about personhood, about relationship and about our own sacred selves. Its purpose is to shine a light upon an area of humanity which is often neglected or stigmatized.

Chapter 1

A Priest's Story

Called to serve

My own particular story starts in the desert, a place of emptiness and isolation. I was a newly ordained curate in Solihull, a large suburban parish in the Diocese of Birmingham. The parish was made up of a team of churches under the mother church, St Alphege. It was a traditional, Anglo-Catholic parish, described as a 'flagship church' by the diocese. I had no previous connection with the West Midlands: I was an Oxford ordinand who had asked to be exported out of the south to somewhere 'north, poor and urban'. Instead, to my surprise, I arrived in the posh part next to Birmingham. The people were high achievers, welcoming, wealthy and expectant. I was to lead these people in the Christian faith; I was to be their preacher, teacher, healer and intercessor. The desert experience began.

The shock of that first year of ordained ministry was something akin to a 180-degree turn. I had been used to enjoying the anonymity of the laity in the pew, a leisurely profession of turning up late, holding prayerful head in hands and receiving all that the Church could offer. The ordained status of deacon meant that my world had to be turned upside down, or at least halfway round. I necessarily had to change from being inconspicuous to being available for, and open to, the people. I did not adapt quickly to becoming a Christian leader. I felt very vulnerable and not a little scared. Such was the disturbance of mind and spirit[1] that I temporarily lost sense of both.

My closest friendships at this time came in the form of a prescription, the standard medical response to ill health. These illusory friends – Prozac and beta-blockers – would serve me well and, after four to six weeks, our relationship became quite intimate. These drugs were for me a pathway to salvation, they gave me hope that I might live as God intended, that I might function as the Church expected, indeed that I might survive. I was referred to a psychiatrist, who confirmed my suspicion that I was feeling a little down. My suspicion had indeed grown and become a focus of its own anxiety. Here was I, a newly ordained deacon of the Church – a servant of the servants of God – devoid of a servant's heart. In simple terms, I was unable to give myself to others. I was unable to concentrate, participate or communicate. I was not able to share my story, or listen to other stories. I could not pray for the world (local and global), or for the people around me, and I was increasingly conscious of the demands that I was making on them. The only prayer uttered was desperate and selfish, 'God, help me.' I felt that I was letting everyone down, and I did not want my fragility, weakness and vulnerability associated with the magisterium of the one, holy, catholic and apostolic Church.

Many in the parish would not have witnessed my disturbance. I fought valiantly to disguise it. But this was a time of crucifixion, a loss of freedom and a loss of self. Many who have been through this experience of depression describe it as a prison. My depression enveloped me as though I were wrapped in a burial cloth like Lazarus, caught in death, unable to escape until Christ's voice was heard in the depth of the tomb. To survive was an ordeal; to attempt to live as a sign of hope for others was impossible. I was receiving psychotherapy at the time, guided by a person of empathy. But this was a long-term therapy, offering no quick fixes. The desert experience of repeated trials and persecutions continued.

This was no new experience. For many years I had been vulnerable to depression and anxiety when embarking upon a new stage of life. It is at such transition times, when change is either self-willed or imposed, that I have myself been disposed to a disturbance of mind and spirit. I had for as long as I can remember experienced episodes of what I later described as 'blacknesses'. As a child I would suffer fairly long periods of emotional instability. My anxiety threshold would be breached especially at times of new beginnings. I remember the terrible fear and worry that a new school year would bring, rudely interrupting the long summer holiday. I did not know that my experiences were any different from those of my classmates. But I knew that these dark, isolated confinements pushed me to try and 'prove' myself to others afresh and anew. I did not want the 'blackness' to overcome me but, at each transition point in my young life, I reacted with bouts of insecurity, somatized through stomach ache and nausea. At such times I felt worthless, incapable of seeing myself in a positive light or being able to contribute to life. This pattern of anxiety preceding change repeated itself on a weekly basis. Sundays became a trial – the worst day of the week – inert, silent, lonely. As I approached adulthood, I experienced more intense periods of melancholia; these times of fragility were nearly always a precursor of a change to my everyday, my world, my comfortable existence.

Today I am conscious of these depressive episodes and the triggers that cause them and their emotional effects. New beginnings are still a key trigger point and, as an adult, different pressures have overtaken the 'new school year' anxiety. Work, marriage, fatherhood, time pressures, mortgage repayments – all have their part to play. My path, occasionally obscured by these 'blacknesses', continues to present challenges. The challenge of entering a new parish (a major new beginning) with its own particular pressures and responsibilities was the catalyst that led to the writing of this book.

A dangerous place

During my curacy the desert did prompt little epiphanies as well which came from exploring the boundaries of self-knowledge. I became particularly immersed in the writings of Henri Nouwen (1994a; 1994b), and his honest self-assessment which highlights our fragile souls and our need to be loved before the broken and fragile heart of God. Nouwen, it seemed, had struggled to fit into the establishment of the Roman Catholic priesthood. His struggle had led him on an uncomfortable journey where he continually sought a homecoming, but was unable to experience it. His was a prolonged disturbance of mind and spirit and one that I was able to identify with. I related to Nouwen as a kindred spirit, and was grateful for his direct testimony. I read his writings knowing that they offered a thread of experience which could haul me out of the pit that I had entered. Nouwen's words suggested that emotional disturbance and unhappiness can be used for good. This was a very pertinent episode in which I was to discover that God may well use the tortured soul. This had been Nouwen's experience also. He received his homecoming in a place quite unexpected to him, in a L'Arche Community[2] where he would end his days.

I made enquiries into leaving the Church, at least on a temporary basis. This would have been a sabbatical year before I had even put six months' duty under my belt. It did not happen, it didn't need to happen, but the prospect was enticing – an avoidance strategy which enabled me to keep a foothold on reality. My twice-weekly psychotherapy, boosted by chemical enhancement gifted by the NHS, occasionally enabled me to peep out of the prison. I believe that this was a time of grace in which creativity played an enormously therapeutic role. I started to paint again, and I began to make connections between suffering, grace and love.

So to my great surprise, the desert was, in reflection, a source of renewable energy and a space that offered the possibility of transform-ation. As the father of faith, Abraham, discovered: 'The desert is a dangerous place. It is always moving, so it is hard to know where you are ... People do not go into the desert unless they have to' (Berryman, 2002, p. 62). I was later to realize that the desert was the literal place of renewal for many Christians in the third and fourth centuries seeking out God. These Christian hermits populated the deserts of Egypt, Syria and Pales-tine and became known as the Desert Fathers and Mothers. They were to initiate a new form of Christian living, later shaped and structured by St Benedict into coenobitic or communal monasticism that was adopted in the West. But the crowd that entered the desert was not a little disturbed in mind and spirit. The sayings of the Desert Fathers are packed with eccentricity, oddity, passion and madness (see Chrysostomos, 1980; Ward, 1981; and Williams, 2003). The lives of the Fathers display strange, inappropriate and boundary-less behaviour that would upset many modern-day perceptions of what a holy life might be. Yet the desert has much to offer in a real, as well as in a figurative sense. So the desert has been a testing ground throughout the story of God's people's quest for community and the story of God's search for his people. God uses the place of desert to form his people. It is a place of extremes where ulti-mately God's love provides the sustenance to survive, and the strength to travel further towards Christ's passion, death and resurrection.

Jesus' own desert pilgrimage somehow resonated with my own expe-rience. His post-baptismal flight into the Jordanian wilderness was the preparation ground for his own ministry, despite the fearful and force-ful attacks of the devil which attempted to prevent him from public service. The desert place which brings us so close to God also brings us into the presence of darkness. In a spiritual sense, this is why the desert is such a dangerous place. In my own cruel desert which had wanted to claim my life, I had also been sorely tested. Christians of the various church traditions name this evil power differently. The evidence of thousands of years of testing is that evil is a reality in the world, and its personality is an enemy of those who seek to know who God is. I believe that the spectrum of mental health on which we all have a place is 'what it is to be human'. I understand that spiritual wars are fought each and every day by seekers of the truth. However, aided by psychological insight we can better understand what it is to suffer from mental ill health.

A new pilgrimage

I was to be given an opportunity to travel out of the desert, to reclaim my ordained journey through companionship and eventually marriage. Jo was training to be a clinical psychologist; she had a strong sense of understanding and well-being. Despite my fragile mental health, we shared a desert view which informed our faith and would later help inform some life decisions together. At our first short meeting, we understood something of our particular roles and shared pilgrimage. A little epiphany had visited the desert of depression and my story was to change into a renewed 'theology of hope' (Moltmann, 1967). I started to understand that not only did I have a place on the mental health spectrum, but that I also had a story to tell, not just of breakdown but of humanity's common vulnerability and strength.

When my four-year curacy was nearing its end, a great deal of energy was expended on the next move. The Church of England has a surprisingly competitive employment market, similar to that of the secular world. A pseudo piety sometimes emerges in certain priestly circles when preferment and ambition are mentioned. Nonetheless, careerism and opportunism are as alive within the Church as they are outside. I was keen to ensure that my ambition correlated with God's ambition for me. It was a difficult process of discernment. Approximately 40 different 'jobs' were tested at one level or another. Jo and I were quite impatient to move, but did our desire meet with God's plans? I was wanting to minister in a place of greater diversity. We sensed that this new beginning might well provide opportunities for our own spiritual formation to develop and deepen.

The parish of Fulham Fields

When the position of parish priest at St Andrew's Church, Fulham Fields, presented itself, I understood that my role there would have a particular emphasis because of the parish's recent traumatic past (namely, the tragic circumstances of its previous incumbent's death). My remit would be, as for all parish priests, wide ranging. For me this would entail building a congregation, developing relationships with other local churches, encouraging the development of the laity, improving the liturgy and maintaining an ageing church building. Above all, though, it seemed I was being asked to be an agent for the healing of the local community. At one level, this task of healing was a unique consequence of my predecessor David's death. At another level, it seemed to have echoes of other parish ministries where, for many and varied reasons, the new incumbent inherits a troubled history. I would not be the first, nor the last, to grapple with themes of loss, bereavement, anger and renewal which would underpin my time there.

After I had accepted the post, the process of endings and new beginnings accelerated. I had for the last 16 months been curate in charge of an interregnum. Life had improved for me and so had my mental health. This renewal had given space and opportunity for the deepening of relationships within the parish. I now felt ready to embark on a new ministry in a very different context. Fulham Fields, located in the Borough of Hammersmith and Fulham in West London, consists of a small parcel of land with a population of approximately 16,000. The city's road and rail arteries run through it. Its physical make-up includes pubs, hospitals, local shops, tower blocks within large council estates, and signs of residential gentrification which are slowly infiltrating the established population. Although geographically compact, life within Fulham Fields would offer social and economic challenges, not to mention cultural and ethnic diversity.

This, then, is the story of our journey to an inner urban parish, made up of a collection of disparate people who regularly gathered together to form a patchwork community representing a varied continuum of strengths, gifts and vulnerabilities. We have set our story in the context of the tragic circumstances which brought a priest and a psychologist from the leafy suburbs of Birmingham to a new place of pastoral encounter.

Chapter 2

A Psychologist's Story

Standing accused

My path to clinical psychology was a rocky one; rocky not least because my journey to qualification was beset with self-doubt, a desire to quit, and some very difficult experiences. Its rockiest patch was, with hindsight, the interview process for training itself. When I was not offered a place on the course of my first choice, I telephoned for feedback. To my dismay, the feedback I received was not a comment on my clinical or academic performance, but rather on my 'integrity'. The concern was raised that I had 'lied' on my application form and, when I tried to defend myself, despite my knowledge that the accusation was unfounded and could be proven so, I found myself floundering.

The matter was, technically speaking, cleared up by an exchange of correspondence between myself, my line manager and the university in question. Nonetheless the effects of this accusation were for me earth-shattering. Until that experience relatively secure in my own mental health, I found myself utterly debilitated by the indictment on my character. Overnight I became tearful, lacking motivation and self-confidence, unable to sleep or eat. Though I had a fortunate escape and my depression lasted a matter of weeks, the incident was a profound one: it left me with a lasting sense that we all of us are vulnerable to fragile mental health; that we all have breaking-points.

When I look back at this period in my life, I remember with immense gratitude the support and affirmation I received from family, friends and several work colleagues. Without this, I know I would not have emerged from the experience so quickly. Nonetheless I struggled to return to a belief in who I was with any conviction. To this day I recall the overwhelming sense of devastation with which this experience left me. I temporarily lost faith, if not in God, then in where it was that he was leading me.

The years have inevitably softened this experience. I now have a more objective understanding of how the accusation probably came about. The university in question, I later learned, had had its fingers burnt a year or so previously by letting someone onto a course who had indeed misrepresented their qualifications. This, combined with my own anxiety in an interview situation, had somehow led to a panel's over-hasty decision to doubt my word and cast judgement on my character. At the time I was incapable of drawing anything positive from the experience. But over the years it has come to hold a critical place in my own personal narrative, one whose meaning, almost without my noticing, has changed over time.

Towards the end of the telephone conversation with the university, having done my best to explain myself, I asked if the misunderstanding would go on to affect my future chances of selection were I to reapply. I was told with little uncertainty, 'No, no, we treat each new intake of applications afresh. That's not to say that people don't have memories.' The inconsistency of this response was probably the lynchpin in my crisis. I felt that, no matter what equal opportunities or fair procedure might maintain, my own story was being written and rewritten for me. Something in that moment of being accused left me shattered. I learned that, when somebody else tries to write your story for you and that version of events has little or no bearing on the truth, it can indeed disturb your mind and your spirit.

The significance of this experience and its relationship to my own role as a mental health practitioner in many ways speaks for itself. Before I even had my first foot on the ladder to clinical psychology training, I was given a profound lesson in what it can mean to take the job of listening lightly and to allow one's own assumptions and experience to get in the way. The somewhat appalling irony of experiencing this from a potential colleague, let alone a very senior one, again is self-evident. And yet it took me some time to start to understand the multiple layers of this experience. The impact on my own mental health was immediate, quickly followed by the unnerving insight into what it is to be mis-understood or misinterpreted. Only later, however, as my training progressed, did I reflect back upon what it meant to be judge and accuser, to take power, wittingly or unwittingly, and use it against another almost without insight into its consequences.

As I have looked back at this episode over the years with increasing distance, it has been relatively easy to ascribe and adhere to my own version of events. Despite the two letters of apology and reassurance that finally came my way, I have tended, if I am honest, to view this episode with a certain degree of self-righteous indignation. After all, I was wrongly accused; the apologies I received were at best faint-hearted, at worst political; the whole episode pointed to a terrible misuse of power. All this is true and I could, I suppose, write these things with some degree of justification. But this adherence on my part to a script that dates back a whole decade seems unhelpful, if not a little 'stuck'. While on this occasion I was the innocent party and a miscarriage of justice did indeed take place, what does the episode say today of my own successes and failures as a clinical psychologist and of my ability as a person to listen or not listen to another's story?

At a professional level, these questions force me to consider my own part in other people's narratives – both colleagues and clients. For example, were a client of mine to read this, would they remember me as someone with whom trust and confidence had never been broken? Or would they remember those occasions when I had been late; when I had not appeared to listen; when perhaps, worst of all, I had somehow used my position in a way that rendered them powerless or highlighted their own fragility? From a perspective of faith, these questions seem to carry me still deeper. What, for example, does my experience of being accused say about the part I have to play in the passion narrative? Might I look back at this historical account with a degree of comfort, confident in the knowledge that I would have behaved differently to 'them': to Pontius Pilate, to Judas, to Peter? Throughout my adolescence and into my early twenties I could never bring myself to join in the crowd's responses to Pilate on Good Friday. I found it hard to listen to the rousing cries of the congregation around me as each person called for the release of Barabbas and gave their voice to 'Let him be crucified! . . . Let him be crucified!' Over the years I have come to recognize my own fear in this scenario; the ease with which we can all displace our individual responsibility onto another – the crowd, 'Doubting Thomas', a senior colleague – and fail to look at our own.

I can indeed recall times when, perhaps feeling out of my depth, or perhaps just tired, I have fallen back on a veil of professionalism to manage a difficult clinical situation. Brian Thorne (2003) writes:

> It is the therapist's privilege to glimpse daily the potential in the human being for self-transcendence . . . Such transformation is not the result, I believe, of the therapist's superior psychological knowledge or even of his or her therapeutic skills. What matters is his or her ability to enter into relational depth where the person seeking help feels profoundly accepted, and where the therapist is perceived as someone who does not hide behind a mask of pseudo-professionalism. (pp. 3–4)

Though professionalism (by contrast with 'pseudo-professionalism') does of course have a vital place, Thorne highlights how it can undermine and invalidate when it comes to replace real respect of one human being for another. The opposite of this is a therapist's profound acceptance of his or her client. This kind of acceptance is what we each of us have a calling to strive for, however far we may fall short of that calling on a daily basis.

It was a very real story of acceptance, of respect and validation, which first led me to clinical psychology.

Finding a vocation

Critical to my decision to embark on my career was my brother's timely, deeply instinctive suggestion, 'I think you should become a child psychologist.' He had just read Virginia Axline's book, *Dibs: In Search of Self* (1964) and passed it on to me. *Dibs* is the story of a young boy who, at the age of five, presents a puzzle and frustration to parents, teachers and professionals alike. Neither speaking nor playing, yet apparently absorbed by his books, others' misperceptions of his personhood have left him utterly isolated. '"He's a strange one"' the paediatrician had said. "Who knows? Mentally retarded? Psychotic? Brain damaged? Who can get close enough to find out what makes him tick?"' (p. 12). This isolation was key to Dibs' withdrawal from everyday communication. In a different way, my own experience of being accused of lying, of having my integrity called into question, similarly pushed me into a place of desolation. Though within weeks I appeared to function normally again, it took me a long time to re-build trust and confidence in others, particularly within what was to become the body of my own profession.

It fell to Axline, a clinical psychologist practising in the USA with an expertise in play therapy, to enter Dibs' world. Through the course of several months, she discovered not only his intense giftedness but also the complexities of his emotional being, driven by a sense that his successful parents did not love him or have time for him. The book details his journey to a place of emotional stability, one that releases Dibs to find out for himself that he is able to manage the contrasts of feelings and experiences that imbibe him.

The final chapter tells of Dibs' request to visit the neighbouring church, visible from the play therapy room. Axline's agreement to this request is unusual, but then, as she herself comments, so is the request. Her description of their excursion seems to push the parameters of their therapeutic relationship into a new territory which combines psychological and spiritual recovery, without imposing it. Axline writes:

We went out of the Centre and walked around the outside of the church. Dibs looked up at it, impressed by its tremendous size.

'Now let's go in. Let's see it inside,' he said.

We went up the front steps. I opened the huge doors and we went inside. Dibs was dwarfed by the lofty archways. He walked slowly down the centre aisle, ran a few steps, stopped, looked up and around him with an expression of complete awe and wonderment on his shining face. He was impressed by the magnificence of the chapel.

'I feel so very, very little,' he said. 'I think I must have shrunk.' He turned slowly and gazed at the beauty around him. . . . Just at that moment, the organist started to play the pipe organ. Dibs ran to me and grabbed my hand.

'Let us go! Let us go! I am afraid!' he cried.

'Did the music frighten you?' I asked, as we started toward the door.

Dibs stopped and looked back. 'Listen. Let's don't go yet,' he said. We stopped.

'I am afraid of the bigness and I am afraid of the noise,' Dibs said. 'But it is so beautiful it fills me with brightness and beauty.'

'Afraid of it, but liking it, too?' I said. 'It is a beautiful church.'

'. . . I have never seen anything so beautiful,' he whispered. The sun was shining through the coloured glass and the beams of light stretched out toward us.

'Let's get out of here,' Dibs said softly. We walked back to the door. Dibs looked back over his shoulder. At the door he stopped again. 'Wait a minute,' he whispered. He waved timidly toward the altar and said in a tiny voice, 'Goodbye, God. Goodbye! (pp. 185–6)

There is something in Dibs' sheer frankness here, both in relation to his feelings about the church and also his communication with God, which is deeply moving. His expression of awe and fear, combined with an inexplicable sense of wonder and beauty, speaks lastingly about that place within each of us which reconciles disturbance and healing.

These lines will no doubt mean something different to each person who reads them. For me, as I read them now, they call to mind my own fragile, often poorly expressed, feelings of vocation. As with Dibs' own journey, this process often has several component parts: leaving a place that is safe and familiar for the unknown; pausing to take stock and reflect before moving forward; and struggling to integrate fear with desire, awe with wonder. Dibs' timid, deeply inspired response to the church has all the honesty and pathos of childhood. With an instinctive understanding of sacred space, he waves timidly towards the altar and says in a small voice, 'Goodbye, God! Goodbye!' It is the simplicity of Dibs' farewell that is so striking: his 'leave-taking' of God is in fact his first direct communication with him.

As I write, I find myself asking why this passage has stayed with me all these years and why I turn to it now in such detail. I think this is because it seems to offer an almost unconscious framework not present in mainstream, psychological thinking today. That is, the passage speaks powerfully about our human existence while allowing for a quiet expression of our sacred selves also. For me, this tentative overlap between a perspective of faith and a psychological one is something of a revelation. While as a clinical psychologist I may feel free in the context of this book to reflect on matters relating to parish life and mental health, in my own work I have always sought to keep my personal beliefs outside the clinical space. Although this feels both appropriate and respectful of a client's own beliefs and ideas, it is also, in a sense, over-simplistic. Our thoughts and actions, however modified, are, if we are to be integrated selves at all, expressions of who we are. As I slowly progress, therefore, through my work and family life, I find I want to seek out a more integrated understanding of myself, one in which faith and psychology more openly play a part.

A meeting of two vocations

Three months into my training, I met Gavin. He had been ordained deacon six months previously and was working as a curate in the West Midlands. As I was living and working in another part of the country, this meeting was at best inconvenient and not what I had bargained for. My placement at the time was in adult mental health. As a first-year trainee, my clinical time was split between primary care and a community mental health team. This meant that, when not at university, I spent part of my working week with clients in a GP practice and the other part with a team of mental health professionals in a psychiatric hospital. These two experiences gave me an initial insight into a varied presentation of mental health in two very different settings.

At this stage in my life, the potentially devastating effects of mental illness had a very powerful place in my own narrative. A close family friend had recently died in tragic circumstances. He had suffered over a number of years from schizophrenia, only latterly diagnosed, and it was his own battle with mental health, combined with the support and courage of his family, which has stayed with me until this day.

When I met Gavin, he confided in me that he was suffering from depression. With an almost concrete determination, he disclosed that he was on anti-depressants, in long-term psychotherapy and in the process of questioning his vocation. His suffering at once troubled and terrified me. I was clear, or so I believed, that of course I could not start a relationship with someone suffering from depression, especially when I was training to be a clinical psychologist. This would seriously call into question the overlap between my personal and professional boundaries. To work or university, however, I took none of this confusion. All the same, my silence forced me into acknowledging my own prejudices about mental health – my fear of others' perceptions, not least, perhaps, because of my own.

In time I have come to realize that a more authentic understanding of the overlap between my personal and professional life is fundamental not only to my own work but also to Gavin's – to our family life and, perhaps I should add, to our tentative yet implicit sense of a shared vocation. This understanding was, I suppose, always there; but it was not really tested until the first move we embarked on together – our journey from Gavin's title parish where he had been curate, to St Andrew's, Fulham Fields, where he became incumbent. This, then, is the story of our three years of living and working in an inner urban parish, Gavin as priest-in-charge at St Andrew's Church and I as a clinical psychologist for a local NHS child development service. It is the story of a brief yet lasting three years, of a time whose significance we hope never to lay to rest. It speaks of our own experiences of mental health in parish ministry and of how these experiences have been informed by a combined theological and psychological perspective.

Integrating Mind and Spirit (Part 1)

Story-telling

Story-telling helps focus our attention on the often complex and sensitive nature of pastoral encounters in parish life. The parish priest is constantly being invited to listen to other people's stories – be this for a baptism or funeral, wedding preparation, hospital visit or perhaps just a chance meeting. The art of listening is by no means an easy one. It is central to a priest's formation but not necessarily to his training. Before we are able to learn from other people's stories, we need to seek to learn from our own: to grapple with our humanity and our own disturbance of mental health.

To recognize our vulnerability is to understand that we each of us have a story to tell. Story-telling in a pastoral context is not, however, a prerequisite for healing in itself, nor should we underestimate the responsibility of this task. Story-telling is not to be held lightly. It is a gift and should be treated so.

Practical implications

Before we can listen meaningfully to the stories of others, we need to have reflected upon and processed our own stories. Below are some practical points which might enable us to do this:

- As individuals with our own needs and vulnerabilities, we need to be mindful of who we tell our story to and how we tell it – when or if we choose to do so.
- As people in positions of pastoral responsibility, it is important to consider the appropriateness of sharing stories with those in need. To what degree does my story help or hinder another person's telling

of his or her own story? If I share my story, will the other person feel their story is being heard?

- It is helpful to hold in mind the tension between our personal and professional lives. For example, how might my own experience of being a mother impact on my role as a clinical child psychologist and vice-versa?
- It is important not to confuse our own stories and experiences with somebody else's – that we do not, for example, assume that the way in which we experience a life situation (for example trauma, bereavement, depression) is how someone else will.
- When seeking to understand our own vulnerabilities and breaking points, we might ask ourselves a few key questions. How have they manifested themselves in the past? What signs might I notice? What might trigger their recurrence/relapse? Who might I go to? How might I protect myself in the future?

Questions for individual reflection and/or discussion

1. What does the term 'mental health' mean to you?
2. What is your own desert story?
3. Consider ways in which God might be revealed to you through the pain and uncertainty of mental and emotional disturbance.
4. What is the value of church leaders, lay and ordained, sharing their stories?

Prayer

God of love,
you share your light with all that you have created.
Your story is to love without condition.
Even in our helplessness, hopelessness and pain you are present.
Draw us to yourself that we may share our story
in the confidence of your abiding mystery:
Father, Son and Holy Spirit. Amen.

Part 2

Frameworks

*In these chapters the four phases of the Eucharist – the Preparation–
Gathering, the Liturgy of the Word, the Liturgy of the Sacrament, and the
Dismissal – are summarized. These phases form a framework which
resonates with the telling of this particular story of mental health in
parochial ministry. This framework is accompanied by a psychological
model of thinking and practice – assessment, formulation, intervention
and evaluation – which may deepen our understanding of the disturbance
of mind and spirit. The combination of these two models will hopefully
facilitate a space for discussion where various levels of narrative are given
the chance to explore the complexities of mental health.*

Parochial
  Ministry

The Preparation

Gathering

The Liturgy of
  the Word

The Liturgy of the
  Sacrament

Psychological
  model of thinking

Assessment

Formulation

Intervention

Evaluation

Chapter 3

The Drama of the Liturgy

Mental health and the liturgy

The Christian story is a story that speaks engagingly about mental health. It is a story that brings mind and spirit into a relationship of disturbance where nothing is certain or guaranteed. On our Christian journey we travel in accompaniment with our fragile and dynamic mental health. There is an element of continuing tension, of unknowing. The Christian story offers hope but not health in a clinical sense. The crucible of our faith – the place within the disturbance of incarnation and resurrection, between Advent and Pentecost – is a place of holiness and mystery, a place of encounter and experience.

The liturgical pattern of the Eucharist is a model of disturbance which may illuminate our own and many other stories. But what is it about the eucharistic pattern, shape and rhythm that somehow connects mind with spirit, and spirit with mind?[1] How can this ancient liturgical rite inform us about the sphere of mental health? It is my belief that the liturgy of the Eucharist is given to God's people for their health and formation. Too often, it seems, especially since the resurgence of the parish communion in the Anglican Church in the 1950s, the Eucharist has been compartmentalized as holy worship for holy people. Its essence, its gift has been hidden or even taken for granted.

The Eucharist is not simply an act of worship but a living story with four integrated dramas within the whole. Each movement has its own *raison d'être*. The component parts of the Eucharist are the Prepara-tion–Gathering, the Liturgy of the Word, the Liturgy of the Sacrament, and the Dismissal. Each speaks profoundly not only about the life of the spirit but also about our human motivations and needs. The living story relates well, therefore, to the complex dimensions of our own health and well-being.

The Eucharist offers an obvious platform on which to project many of the challenges that our inner worlds present. Each of its four movements incorporates particular aspects of life that demand theological reflection. The following chapters will venture to open up the possibility that the gift of the Eucharist offers many pathways to God, especially the disturbing path towards self-knowledge.

*   *   *

The Eucharist represents the paradox upon which the Church is founded – that new life is created through brokenness. Jesus shared a meal with his friends and followers celebrating the Passover, the liberation of the Hebrew people from their Egyptian captors. This meal of freedom was the preface of Christ's passion. This meal, which foretells the human traits of betrayal and denial (from Judas and Peter), also gave opportunity for the richest display of human charity – the washing of the disciples' feet by God himself. The Last Supper not only acts as a memorial of the most sacred of meals for Christians, but it also represents the meeting place between what it is to be human (weak, vulnerable and tempted) and what it is to be holy (to partake in God's will).

Imagine the levels of human emotion that were present in the upper room. Imagine the degrees of disturbance that were unsettling the group of brothers. Mental illness was not a recognized condition in the first century. Psychology is a relatively modern discipline. Yet I wonder what emotional and social pressures members of the group experienced? These pressures were products of the human condition, our shared condition, broken and outpoured, not exclusively revealed to a few but the divine substance of our lives.

Public work

The original meaning of the Greek reveals that liturgy is defined as 'public work of any kind',[2] and this meaning has developed into a sense of God's work being done for and with the people of God. Thus, through the liturgy, Christ continues the work of salvation through his Church. The definition has echoes of my own personal vocation into the priesthood and my desire, however thwarted, to serve not only the Church but the world in which I live. I understand that the Church of God cannot be disconnected from the world that God created. This is the ground rock of my faith. My vocation as priest has therefore got everything to do with all of God's creation. The liturgy is the working out of this relationship between the Church and the world. It is the public work of God, the interaction between light and dark, liberation and captivity, wholeness and brokenness.

The Eucharist, a thanksgiving meal for the sacrifice of Christ and his victory over death, also emphasizes contradictory themes of passion, thanksgiving, darkness and hope which have echoes of mental health stories. Many people who have experienced depression refer to it as a type of prison. The mind becomes captive, darkened to the prospect of escape and freedom. Many of the people of St Andrew's have lived this living death – some quietly in isolation, others openly and hopelessly, but all living Christ's passion.

The Eucharist is pivotal to my belief that, at the moment of brokenness, we can lose sight of purpose or meaning; but that, as we move towards an understanding of our brokenness, then healing can take place. It is the basis of all liturgical worship, transforming hearts and minds, making the living Christ present in our captivity, releasing us from the terrors of denial, betrayal and the loss of love. This is the institution of Christ, sanctified by God. It offers order and structure. It repeats words and phrases unashamedly throughout the Christian centuries. And the story that is told again and again to generation upon generation is a sign of God's continuing presence. God is not only interested in us, he calls us to share his life. So the Eucharist sings of timeless praise in the midst of human disorder and social dysfunction. St Paul explains that, through this public work, this holy worship, we are not con-formed to this age but trans-formed through God's grace:

> I appeal to you therefore, brothers and sisters, by the mercies of God, to present your bodies as a living sacrifice, holy and acceptable to God, which is your spiritual worship. Do not be conformed to this world, but be transformed by the renewing of your minds, so that you may discern what is the will of God – what is good and acceptable and perfect. (Romans 12.1–2)[3]

The order of the Eucharist is, therefore, a place of strong resistance to the strictures of modern-day living. It offers a beginning and an end in a constant rhythm. It offers a place in which to rest burdens and ills, and it provides space for the truth to be heard. It empowers those who believe in the possibility of being transformed and guides them into this new life together.

At one particular stage of my life, when I was battling against God's calling to the ordained ministry, I struggled to see the relevance of the Church in today's society. I did not know what function worship and praise played in the Church's mission. I saw the vulnerability and fragility of the Church as a weakness rather than a strength. I found it hard to understand that the Church was called to be a healing presence. Despite this, one of the most tangible exhibitions of the Church's healing was presented to me during a half-hour lunchtime healing service. The church was scattered with a handful of strangers, from a tiny corner of London. It was bathed in an atmosphere of good intent. The lost, the sick and the lame were welcomed into the arms of love. Nothing much happened. Hands were laid on, people were anointed with oil, prayers were said. Nothing much happened, yet transformation lay at the heart of this service, this simple liturgy which expressed the story of the Eucharist; that Christ shares our loss, our sickness and our pain.

I was brought up in a low evangelical church where Holy Communion was offered only once a month. Nonetheless both the place and the people helped root me in my baptismal faith and gave me a lasting insight into church life. As I grew up, this early foundation of faith encouraged me to explore different forms of Christian worship that exuded warmth, colour and passion. In time I discovered a more sacramental form of worship: mystical, reverential and deeply symbolic. During my battle against ordination, I dreamt of serving in a church that was bathed with theatre and colour. During the process of interpreting these experiences, I became aware that I was entering into the passion of Christ, understanding that good liturgical practice somehow led me into the journey of Calvary and, beyond that, the Easter tomb. It bore witness to the human struggle for what St Paul called 'the freedom that we have in Christ' (Galatians 2.4).

This was my experience, and I continue to be fed by liturgy in various ways. Of course, this is not always my experience; nor is it the experience of many others. But nonetheless the Eucharist speaks to me, it gives meaning to my life and the lives of those I care for and minister to. It is, I believe, the dance of life. This, then, is a narrative which seeks to explore further the way in which the Eucharist relates to the parish and especially those within it who seek health and understanding.

A memorial

The Eucharist is central to the life of worship at St Andrew's, Fulham Fields. It was central to the life and ministry of David Paget, Vicar of St Andrew's Church. He celebrated the Eucharist daily. He took, blessed, broke and shared the body and blood of Christ with whoever was present. After David's death a memorial fund was set up by St Andrew's Parochial Church Council (PCC), at this time led by the churchwardens. The aim of the fund was to register somehow the grief of all those who David served in his earthly ministry. David's murder had caused shock and outrage. Some parishioners were so haunted by the tragedy that they were unable to step into the church after his death. Others could be heard at times to comment, as they walked past the vicarage, on the events which had taken place there.

Enough money was eventually raised by the local community, many of whom were not churchgoers, to commemorate creatively David's life and ministry. The main proceeds went towards a window on the north transept, adjacent to the nave altar where, aptly, the sacrificial meal was consecrated. The design for the memorial was deliberately endorsed with a eucharistic theme: grapevines denoting the wine of the holy feast and wheatsheaves symbolizing the bread. It was a simple emblem which attempted to portray the gifts that God's creation offers.

The Eucharist, like any sacrament, speaks of transformation, and it was intended that the window would demonstrate something of the journey from our human need and brokenness into the unity of the divine. Many of the windows around the church had been smashed and vandalized after the news of David's death reached the local youth. The institutional Church is vulnerable to such disturbance. It offers little protection or safety for its clergy, its people or its buildings. But how can it? The Church does not claim to be a place of comfort or safety; the earliest believers are witnesses to that. The window that was most damaged was to become the Father David Memorial Window. It seemed to reflect something of the parish's brokenness and its need for healing.

David's death motivated an angry response. A year or so after my licensing I found many of the stones which had been used as missiles of destruction in among the organ pipes. The window was repaired and renewed.

The Bishop of Kensington came to bless and dedicate the window and David's family was invited to attend. We were all able to share our stories after the service during a bring-and-share lunch. There was much laughter and not a little sorrow. Fragile mental health was a significant aspect of David's ministry to others. Mental health continued to disturb the parish of Fulham Fields. The damaged window is one metaphor for the parish's brokenness and vulnerability; yet the elements of the Eucharist in the bread and wine were to become symbols of hope and resilience.

A pastoral encounter

The liturgy of the Eucharist mysteriously articulates the connection between God's continuing story of salvation and our own story of belief, denial and need. The rite of penitence is placed at the beginning of the liturgy. This placement is out of necessity. We need to right the wrongs that we have done. We need to see ourselves in a true perspective in the context of God's forgiveness and grace. As the people gather and prepare to be inspired by God's word and transformed by Christ's sacrament, the waiting and searching, the desiring for God's life, awakens in prayer. In terms of liturgical process, an introit hymn is sung in order to emphasize that holy worship is commencing. The people are greeted by the priest as a representative of Christ on earth. God's time is now replacing human endeavour. The theme of the particular celebration, the time or the season, is hopefully conveyed by the words of the hymns sung throughout the service.

Silence is key in this waiting time as the people prepare to listen to God's word. But what has waiting and preparing to do with the pastoral encounter that takes place in this sacramental disturbance? The different movements of the Eucharist represent a personal and a collective encounter with the life of God. This is what I understand as the pastoral encounter where we as human beings are accepted entirely for who we are. We are given opportunity to give our whole selves to God in sacrifice as he gives himself to us. We do not choose God but God chooses us;[4] he yearns for our life in relationship with his. The pastoral encounter that is manifested in the eucharistic celebration is the only time in life when we are conscious that we are unreservedly accepted for who we are, that we are known. The surprise of this encounter is that God calls us by our names, calls us to continue the dance of life, the dance that knows no end.

Every time that I prepared to celebrate the Eucharist at St Andrew's I did not know how many of the people would be present, or who some of the people were. Celebrating the Eucharist is always a chance encounter. One thing would be sure, however: that the people waiting and preparing for the celebration would be in need of care. Sometimes this need would be articulated, at other times it would be an unspoken desire. At St Andrew's the need for care was more openly recognizable.

The distribution of Communion at St Andrew's took place with the congregation forming a circle around the altar. The baptized children also received the sacrament, an Orthodox tradition adopted by David portraying his own inclusive theology. In the circle of faces I could see many familiar friends, and one or two new to our family. As I am caught in this moment of possibility with the body and blood of Christ present for all to receive, I am able to recall some of the many who have contributed to the church's life at St Andrew's: Jad, who stands outside the circle when receiving the sacrament; Pip, who draws attention to herself during the choir's anthems by beating a rhythm on the pew in front of her; Annette, who is scared of people, and is doing well to be in church on a Sunday; Darren, who has almost entirely lost the capacity to speak. The pastoral encounter is both personal and common. It is a celebration because, despite our health, status or age, God calls us to be transformed more closely into his image. St Andrew's was a real example of this model of disturbance. My hope is that the succeeding chapters will illuminate the reader's mind and spirit to understand something of the divine disturbance that the liturgy enacts.

Yet this is a difficult story to tell; it is a difficult story to hear. It would be almost impossible to understand if we hadn't gathered as a community, heard the word of God and touched the sacrament of Christ and been sent out into the world together. Liturgy empowers the Church to tell, touch and hear the most difficult story and somehow incorporate it into the substance of our own lives. We have inherited this liturgy from centuries of prayer and worship, study and conflict. This is the gift that the Church has received today from countless Christian journeys of the past. It is a living gift for the people of God, a gift which continues to be the most creative way to tell the most difficult story.

The liturgy is the story of the eucharistic offering through its birth-pangs of penitence, its revelation of God's word and the healing power of God's presence in the sacrament. This book explores the offering of Christians in countless parishes who dedicate their lives to God in prayer and in deed. David's death was a tragedy for the church and its people and it spoke of the danger of living out the priestly life. This then was the offering of my predecessor, a friend I never knew in life.

It was in the parish of Fulham Fields that the public work of the liturgy was lived out alongside the public news of David's death. Where many would fear to tread in the shadow of such 'bad news', the Church continued its dedicated ministry to the people of the parish. The rhythm of life was to carry on, the order of the liturgy continued to speak out the Easter promise: 'Christ has died, Christ is risen, Christ will come again.'[5]

Chapter 4

Mapping Out Clinical Psychology

Good liturgies are like helpful psychological aids to growing in a spiritual relationship.

(Savage and Watts, 2002, p. 25)

Liturgy and clinical psychology

In July 2002, I joined Gavin and a group of fellow curates from the Birmingham Diocese in taking a party of 'young people' to Taizé, a community of brothers in rural Burgundy, south-east France. Some several thousand under-thirties flock to Taizé each year on a pilgrimage to search out their faith and share it with others. The life is one of simplicity and inclusivity. Ecumenism lies at the heart of the brothers' fellowship.

We had been in Taizé a week and it was our last morning. The sun beat down on us and the grass where our tents had been pitched showed tawny patches. Cross-legged or kneeling, we formed a small circle on the burnt turf: six friends in all, we were a mixture of curates and spouses, and the decision to celebrate the Eucharist had been impromptu. Preparations for the celebration were brief. We had no service book to hand, but someone had brought a Bible. We had some left-over wine from the night before, a plastic cup and a baguette. It was enough. Celebration was shared out between Gavin and two fellow curates. Between them they were able to lead us through the liturgy and, in the melée of tents, farewells and laughter, we were able to follow. I remember receiving the cup and being almost surprised to do so. I drank from it: not the careful Anglican sip I had unconsciously rehearsed through the years, but a proper, whole-hearted glug. The wine must have been past its best.

Certainly the bread was stale. Some 18 years confirmed, it felt like my first Communion.

*   *   *

It was not until several months into our first year at St Andrew's that I started to understand a little of what was meant by 'liturgy'. The four movements of the liturgical pattern were a complete mystery to me. I had been experiencing them, if not week in, week out, then year in, year out for as long as I could remember. The discovery, therefore, that I had been engaging in these four movements – Preparation–Gathering, the Liturgy of the Word, the Liturgy of the Sacrament, and the Dismissal – quite unawares, was something of a Eureka moment. Aside from highlighting my utter ignorance, it seemed to bring into relief my passive attention to text (and drama) in a church setting. As a sometime English student and clinical psychologist, this is perhaps nothing to boast about. And yet it seems to go hand in hand with my appalling sense of direction: I can go somewhere again and again but, for as long as someone else is in charge of the route, I have no idea where I am going. The analogy has something akin to the practice of clinical psychology. From a client's perspective, it may well seem that the substance of our sessions is an almost random process. It would be hard to detect, with an untrained ear or eye, any particular framework guiding the conversations and patterns that evolve. And yet, as with liturgy, there is a very definite framework which underpins a clinical psychologist's conceptual thinking: namely, the process of assessment, formulation, intervention and evaluation.

Psychological assessment to evaluation

The process of psychological assessment through to evaluation is not a linear one, but it is useful to think of it in linear terms to begin with. The assessment stage is, as you would expect, the starting point for the relationship between clinical psychologist and client. When I meet with a client and possibly his or her family members for the first time, my aim is to find out what it is that has brought them to this place: the concerns, worries and stories that have led to their presenting difficulties. Having established something of a client's understanding about why they are there, I am keen to discover *why now*: that is to say, what particular events have led up to their referral at this point in time. I am also likely to ask how far back the problem goes. If the client were to chart the problem, what peaks and troughs would they see? What beliefs and thoughts do they have about the problem? What coping strategies or resources have they already tried? What, if anything, appears to help? How would they know they were getting better? Who else is in the individual's network, family, friends, or professional, and to what extent do they find this supportive?

My line of questioning is determined by the client's story as it evolves and by my own understanding of the themes or patterns that underpin this story. If I am concerned, for example, that the mother of a child with behavioural problems is herself depressed, I am likely to ask a series of questions about the mother's own mood. Timing here is essential, not least because of the importance of engaging with the client in the first instance. Asking after a parent's mood in the first session may or may not be appropriate, and may or may not be engaging.

Either way, it is through this dialogue that I am able to deepen my understanding of the presenting problem and wider issues. It is this understanding – these initial ideas – that underpins my psychological formulation of a client's history. The formulation is, then, an evolving explanation of their difficulties. It is not generated by me alone but ideally is a collaborative process between client and psychologist. Furthermore, it is not set in stone but is constantly changing as themes and stories evolve. An initial formulation of a client's difficulties will quickly be re-formulated, and this process will take place again and again.

The formulation goes on to inform how best to work with that client – in other words, it guides the psychological intervention that will follow. This intervention has the potential for several dimensions. In the child and family example used above, it may not be appropriate to engage the parents in thinking about strategies to help manage the child's behaviour until the issue of the mother's depression has been addressed. Or it might be appropriate to work with these two issues concurrently. If the mother's depression is of particular concern, referral to another agency is of course a possibility too.

Last but not least is the process of psychological evaluation: that is, looking back and evaluating the validity of our formulations and the effectiveness of our interventions. To what extent have the presenting difficulties improved? How might the interventions themselves be improved? How shall we address the question of relapse? In other words, should the difficulties re-emerge, how might the client recognize that there is a problem? What skills and which people might they draw upon to help themselves more readily? As with the process of formulation, evaluation is not a linear function but works dynamically. Evaluation of our work is not saved until the final therapy session. It is essential that we evaluate the therapeutic process throughout.

In summary, the process of assessment, formulation, intervention and evaluation informs a clinical psychologist's everyday psychological thinking. It invites us to stand back, slow down and reflect on our clinical work. The framework is rooted in evidence-based practice: that is, a body of theory and research which seeks to validate our understanding of mental health and 'what works for whom' (Roth and Fogarty, 1996). This practice incorporates a range of psychological models including behavioural and cognitive–behavioural models as well as psychodynamic models. In addition, although systemic theory does not fully ally itself with this process, it is also central to a clinical psychologist's work. The many dimensions of a clinical psychologist's framework reflect the very complexities of mental health and human vulnerability. They allow us to engage in flexible thinking which is intrinsic to the complexities of multidisciplinary working – and, it seems to me – parish life.

Clinical psychology training

Preparation for the complexities of mental health begins with training. Clinical psychology training is a protracted one and, in my case, the detour was slightly longer. Having graduated in English, I then set about pursuing a part-time conversion course into psychology. During this two-year period, I initially gained some voluntary work experience with the mental health charity MIND. For six months, on a weekly basis, I worked with a group of elderly people in a day-care centre: some with dementia or Alzheimer's disease, others physically frail, so the centre provided its carers with much-needed respite; some bereaved and wanting company. After this six-month period, I moved across to a day centre for adults with long-term mental health problems. As with the group of elderly, here I helped organize and participate in the group's activities, I talked with them, drank tea with them and ate lunch with them. I understood little of their difficulties but they welcomed me and

I felt I was part of their community. With hindsight, these two experiences, characterized by the rhythmic cycle of weekly fellowship, had much in common with parish life.

Once I had completed my conversion course, I worked for a year as an assistant psychologist. During the course of these 12 months, I worked across two NHS trusts in a range of child and family and mental health settings. Clinical psychology training is a three-year course. As a trainee I was attached to a university which provided my academic training and organized my placements in a range of settings in the NHS. I was therefore employed and funded by the local NHS trust. The structure of training has changed in recent years but in the late 1990s it was divided into four main areas according to client group: child and family, adult mental health, learning disabilities and older adults (or elderly). Each of these areas constituted a six-month placement during the course of years one and two. In the third year, we had the option of selecting specialist placements. My two 'specialisms' were child psychotherapy and children with autistic spectrum disorder. As child psychotherapy is, however, a life's work and I merely dabbled my feet for a few months, I use the term 'specialism' with extreme caution and in the context of training only.

Mental health and parish life

Over the years I have been privileged to experience the richness and breadth of a clinical psychologist's role to varying degrees. To try to describe this richness would be a thankless task. Psychological difficulties and vulnerability clearly vary across the lifespan but no section of life is impervious. In infancy and early childhood, difficulties can include sleep, eating and behavioural problems. In middle childhood and adolescence, other problems come into focus, including attention and hyperactivity problems, anxiety, depression, eating disorders, early onset schizophrenia and substance misuse. Some of these problems might continue into or first find expression in adulthood. Others might belong firmly to a given epoch. Either way, it goes without saying that these difficulties do not exist in isolation but are played out in the context of family difficulties, socio-economic and cultural difficulties. Bereavement, separation, divorce, trauma of any kind, emotional, sexual and physical abuse, the experience of being bullied – all can be contributing factors to a breakdown in mental health.

How, therefore, do we begin to describe the multiple vulnerabilities expressed by our human condition? Physical disability, learning disability, old age, adolescence, chronic illness, developmental disorders, Alzheimer's disease and other dementias – the list is endless. Some vulnerabilities reach clinically diagnostic thresholds. Others might simply be perceived as the everyday stressors of human life. How this potential is realized will vary, of course, according to a combination of internal and external factors: our internal robustness, say, combined with our support network, socio-economic advantage and genetic make-up. Whichever way you look at it, these vulnerabilities are not uniquely expressed in psychological and psychiatric services. They are played out in all walks of life, not least parish life where, ideally, human frailties are allowed to emerge in a safe and non-judgemental environment.

*   *   *

It is hoped, in the chapters to follow, that a liturgical perspective of mental health, and a psychological perspective of liturgy, will emerge. While, as far as we are aware, a combined approach of these two perspectives is new territory, Savage and Watts have already drawn our attention to the relationship between psychology and liturgy in 'The Psychology of Church Services':

> How different people respond to the Communion, or indeed whether it affects them at all, will depend to some extent on their psychological style and capacities. It requires them to engage both emotionally and intellectually, and to hold those two aspects of their response together. It requires them to draw deeply from their own experience, to relate to those around them, and to reach out to God, and again to hold all of these together. (Savage and Watts, 2002, p. 25)

In the light of this, it seems only natural that an individual's mental health – his potential for both brokenness and healing – might find expression in two key frameworks: liturgical and psychological.

Integrating Mind and Spirit (Part 2)

Frameworks

Both liturgy and psychology offer frameworks which encourage safe, bound-aried and contained practice. These frameworks, tried and tested over generations, are not personality led but should speak for themselves. The liturgical process does not need to be intellectually understood in order to be experienced meaningfully. Rather, it invites each and every one of us to experience its many parts at both an individual and corporate level. In this way the liturgy of the Eucharist has the potential to speak to the vast spectrum of humanity and, within this spectrum, to our individual levels of disturbance.

When our mental health breaks down, the rhythm and structures of our everyday lives are often the first thing to go. In those moments, therefore, when we are at our most vulnerable, our most broken, the call to the Eucharist is powerful testimony to our need for rhythm, continuity and containment. It is the priest's task to continue this rhythm beyond the confines of the church building into the wider context of his ministry. Strengthened by the sacramental framework, the priest is better equipped to respond to the multiple needs – sometimes chaotic, sometimes daunting – of parish life.

Practical implications

In the context of parish life, the creation of holy space need not be limited to public worship. The church needs to promote a sense of containment beyond the confines of the Eucharist. It can be helpful to recognize the value of what one's church is already doing, as well as considering some new ways that might achieve this:

- By providing support immediately after the Eucharist for those who have been affected in some way during the service.
- By providing a sense of sanctuary, for example by communicating something of the Eucharist through the presence of the Blessed Sacrament, the use of icons, votive candles, the opened book of the Gospels, even music.
- By developing a lay rota that creates a sense of welcome and security throughout the course of the week. This might include the existing infrastructures of the church (for example flower arranging, cleaning) as well as more formal structures such as church tour guides or, if at all possible, even a lay chaplaincy team.

Questions for individual reflection and/or discussion

1. How can the liturgical framework of the Eucharist inform our lives? How might other frameworks, structures and routines provide resources for living?
2. Which parts of the liturgy have the deepest meaning for you? Why might this be?
3. In what ways can the liturgy help you reflect on your experiences of brokenness and/or healing?
4. What does your church already do to create a contained space for its parishioners? What might it do to improve this?

Prayer

God of wonder, you beckon us to live life in all of its fullness.
In simple trust we explore ways to respond.
Give us courage and strength to find a simple 'Yes.'
Made in your image, help us to accept who we are in mind and
    spirit,
that we may serve each other in the path that leads to wholeness.
Amen.

Part 3

Starting Out

The following two chapters will consider how both the Preparation–Gathering and Psychological Assessment highlight the importance of preparing well in two different settings, liturgical and psychological. This is particularly significant in the fragile contexts of the eucharistic community and of working in mental health.

From a liturgical perspective, the Preparation–Gathering marks the arrival of the worshipping community. It presents the worshipper with a contained space dedicated to stilling both frenetic activity and intellectual busy-ness. It is a time in which the individual makes the first steps of the liturgical journey towards communion with God. When we prepare ourselves for the Eucharist we are asked to seek forgiveness from God through confession and receive the freedom of absolution. The story of the preparation is a story of beginnings, new life, new possibilities, renewed faith.

This process of preparation, gathering, confession and absolution also finds expression in a clinical psychology assessment. Once the people have gathered (clinical psychologist, individuals, family), the key individual(s) are invited to tell their story. This story is in one sense like a confession – not a confession of sins, but a confession of worries, strengths, beliefs and events which have led them to this point of referral. Though clearly no Absolution is given here, sometimes simply the experience of telling this story (and knowing you are heard) is releasing in itself. This first phase acts, then, as it does in the liturgical context, as important preparation ground from which the healing process can evolve.

Chapter 5

The Preparation–Gathering

A confession of faith

When a new incumbent arrives in a parish there are two alternative courses of action to be taken: sit back and reflect upon the place and the people before introducing any changes, or immediately to make changes which would determine one's own style of ministry. I chose the latter, not for a lack of prayerfulness but as a matter of necessity. I had inherited a eucharistic rite which was a hybrid of various denominational theologies. David had been influenced by Roman Catholic and Orthodox ecclesiology and had translated that interest into an individually 'customized' liturgy. At the time, the Anglican Church was celebrating the new dawn of *Common Worship* and, as a new incumbent, I was keen not to transgress Canon Law. I was concerned literally to make the Eucharist more common, inclusive and understood. I wanted to offer a space where all could share, where all hearts and minds could bring something to the celebration.

The gathering at St Andrew's attracted an incredibly diverse crowd. This contrasted with many neighbouring churches which displayed the demographic trait of 'like attracting like'. St Andrew's congregation represented the most remarkable cross-section of twenty-first-century Britain. That was the joy of being a parish priest in the inner urban setting of Fulham Fields – a joy and a challenge.

The church's creed of inclusivity and openness created occasion for idiosyncratic behaviour and emotional outbursts. I attempted to deal with inebriated visitors more often than I would have liked. One such visitor camped down in the Lady Chapel before the Reserved Sacrament and, in his drunken slumber, urinated on himself and the pew. The remaining odour of the threadbare carpet continued to remind us of his stay. He was most apologetic when I awoke him. He had been to St Andrew's before and he would visit again. Even the formality of a well-structured liturgy could not act as a shield to deflect the interruptions of those struggling to express themselves outside the church building. Their psychological fragility did not change as a result of being inside the sacred space. The church was a safe place in which to exercise fearful concerns and latent worries. St Andrew's attracted many who were disturbed and vulnerable.

I had therefore two crucial and interrelated objectives as I prepared to start my journey with this particular company of believers: first, that I might offer some sense of containment and stability in the aftermath of their trauma and fear; second, that I might offer through the beauty and depth of eucharistic worship an opportunity for the parish to travel from Good Friday to Easter Day.

My initial meetings with the churchwardens, area dean and bishop pre-warned me about the divisions that were present in the parish. These divisions had a particular catalyst which stemmed from the press reports of David's death. Upon his death, David acquired many personas including saint, martyr, son and best friend. These positive images were undermined by reactionary, at times negative voices in the parish which had the effect of splitting the congregation. These reactions to David's death provoked a pastoral disturbance which needed diocesan intervention from the area bishop and the area dean to placate. Repentance and confession were greatly needed as anger, betrayal and guilt continued to surface throughout the interregnum.

I decided to write a letter to the parish on the occasion of the first anniversary of David's death. I was not yet licensed to the parish, but I felt the need to engage with the parish, to prepare for the start of my ministry. I wrote the letter on the Feast of Corpus Christi, a coincidental moment in time when Christ's story integrated at a practical human level with the parish's story of brokenness and healing. I wanted to encounter the pain that had visited the parish, to be sensitive to their loss and reflect upon the strengths of David's ministry. The letter aimed to convey both sympathy and empathy, the two forms of pathos which parallel the Feast of Corpus Christi. The significance of Corpus Christi for catholic Christians is that the sacrifice of Christ is given to the world as a life-giving memorial. The feast of the Eucharist, Christ's body and blood, are the sacramental elements that give 'pardon, healing, gladness [and] strength' (Milner-White, 1966, cited by Burnham, 2001, p. 315). The sacrament of the Eucharist, God's most generous and lasting gift to us, guides us to the path of gratitude and healing. Could I perhaps impart this thought and make some sense of David's death, which seemed to many so senseless? David, a priest of God's Church who presided over the Eucharist daily, would have fully understood the meaning behind the message: no life is lost in Christ. My letter was intended as a gentle reminder that God redeems all things to himself.

This work of redemption is a dialogue of care between God and his people. It was becoming clear to me that there was much redemptive work to be done. I wanted the parish to face the future with hope as well as being able to reflect on the past with thanksgiving. The Collect for Corpus Christi describes this journey of redemption that Christ offers in the Eucharist:

> Lord Jesus Christ,
> we thank you that in this wonderful sacrament
> you have given us the memorial of your passion:
> grant us so to reverence the sacred mysteries
> of your body and blood
> that we may know within ourselves
> and show forth in our lives the fruits of your redemption;
> for you are alive and reign with the Father
> in the unity of the Holy Spirit,
> one God, now and for ever.[1]

Whenever a new priest is appointed to a church in the Anglican Communion, he is not supposed to attend worship in that place before being licensed by the bishop. The protocol is not always observed! After moving into the vicarage opposite the church, I sneaked into the nave where about 50 people sat in their pews. I was purposefully a little late in arriving, but I was not the only one. I found out later that punctuality was not considered a priority by many at St Andrew's. Many of my much-loved parishioners would habitually arrive in time for the Gospel or even later in some cases. As my knees settled awkwardly upon the hassock, I became aware of those around me whom I would minister to and who would minister to me. My first impressions were key to my future ministry. This was my first real preparation for my impending incumbency. I was aware of the atmosphere of the church – light, airy, full of potential and possibility. This was the last time that I would be able to gain such a leisurely perspective of the people of St Andrew's, Fulham Fields, and the liturgy that served them.

My training incumbent had advised me some years before that the step from curate to incumbent was the most difficult to make in the Church's hierarchical framework. He was right. The experience of curacy in a caring, praying church presents a very different challenge from the experience of incumbency where hard decisions have to be made, challenges presented and conflicts and upsets confronted. My increasing anxiety was natural enough – how could I be a healing presence to these people? I was neither prepared nor skilled for the task. I felt naked at the prospect of shepherding this community. In the ensuing days before my licensing I prayed for God's grace, guidance and strength in order that I might be prepared to hear the parish's story and, through the hearing of the story, be a priest to the people.

I was licensed to the parish on the Feast of the Commemoration of Theodore of Tarsus. Theodore was a brilliant seventh-century strategist. After his preferment from sub-deacon to Archbishop of Canterbury, he set about modernizing the Church in England. He gave order to the Church through his creation of diocesan governance and by giving clergy and monks a sense of accountability. My licensing, therefore, took place on a day which commemorates a man of renewal and order. This was a holy coincidence and provoked a great deal of laughter. Yet my ministry at St Andrew's needed Theodore's strategic vision to set about the renewal of St Andrew's Church, Fulham Fields.

When the licensing took place, my new bishop invited me to meet David's mother. The churchwardens were keen to invite her to the licensing because they wanted to convey the message that David's ministry was to continue during my incumbency, albeit in a different way. Our meeting was a pivotal moment for me as I became conscious of the pain and loneliness of this mother's grief. I also became aware of the parish's love for David and grief at his loss. The meeting was a sort of confession, a time when reality seems to become clearer through truthful discourse. The living out of this form of confessional faith was, of course, a longer-term project, but I felt a great joy at the licensing service. It was as though the service acted like a form of absolution for me and the parish, a granting of permission to continue the work of Christ without some of the terrible burdens that had overwhelmed the church as a result of David's death.

Perhaps the most significant factor in preparing to shepherd my new flock was an intuition that the people of St Andrew's desired to reap the fruits of God's redemption. The way forward, I trusted, was through the rite of Confession. Such was their confusion over the loss of their shepherd that a great deal of confidence and hope had been lost. How can we 'know within ourselves' God's hope for us when we ourselves are hope-less? The suddenness of David's death appeared to have left much unresolved, at least in the short term. Its traumatic nature left people uncertain, paralyzed even, about how to articulate their grief, their sense of loss and regret. For me this highlighted an underlying need for the parish to communicate something of the truth about their experience of David's death in a safe and boundaried way. The rite of Confession, grounded in church practice and tradition, seemed a natural and appropriate starting point. Confession, I hoped, would help promote some redemptive fruits.

I had feared that a call to Confession was unlikely to reach its hearers if it was imposed. If, however, it could be gently woven into the worship structure, the community might waken to the possibility of God's forgiveness. This process is described, as the title suggests, in *Confession: Doorway to Forgiveness*:

> Repentance . . . is the recognition that I cannot live any more as I have been living, because in living that way I wall myself apart from others and from God. Repentance is a change of direction. Repentance is the door of communion. (Forest, 2002, p. 10)

This broken communion was in great need of healing and restoration. The community was not in the right place to encounter the word of God or be present to the presence of God in the sacrament. Change, transformation and transition were called for throughout this church if it aspired to be called 'one, holy, catholic and apostolic' (the Nicene Creed).

It is necessary, therefore, that the penitential rite speaks to God's people about moving on, adapting, growing, changing. This is demonstrated by the *Common Worship* prayer of confession:

Most merciful God, Father of our Lord Jesus Christ, we confess that we have sinned, in thought, word and deed. We have not loved you with our whole heart. We have not loved our neighbours as ourselves. In your mercy forgive what we have been, help us to amend what we are and direct what we shall be; that we may do justly, love mercy, and walk humbly with you, our God.

My preparation and our gathering in this inner urban parish encouraged me to reflect on my own personal story and, at a pastoral level, on all the particular events which emerged from David's death. This reflection included some very direct 'God help me' prayers. I also felt that grace was invoked through my own sense of limitation. In this way I felt better placed to listen to the traumatic story of the parish with empathy and compassion. In other words, I was now more equipped to handle the parish's history while at the same time trying to put my own issues to one side.

Creating space for God

How can the rite of Preparation–Gathering help us when 'we have not loved you with our whole heart [and when] we have not loved our neighbours as ourselves'? How can the rite inform our sense of discipleship when the disciples are suffering from such a disturbance of mind and spirit? As the name suggests, those who enter church prepare themselves to receive God in word and sacrament. This is a communal event, public in its very nature; anyone and everyone is welcome to join; no membership badge is required. The church of St Andrew's was very keen to engage with the world outside its walls. The church remained open during the day, despite theft, signs of arson and vandalism. We also proudly promoted this notice in our literature:

St Andrew's is a church where people are called to come together to explore the mystery of God's love. We listen to the Word of God and celebrate Christ among us in the Eucharist. After our fellowship we are sent back into the world in a spirit of faith, hope and love. All of us, without exception, are called by God. We welcome you.

Stephen Cottrell (2001) recognizes the community element of assembling together in the Preparation–Gathering rite. A time of transition occurs upon entering the church and meeting with friends and strangers alike. Cottrell asserts that 'we might gather right, knowing who we are, what we are about and where we are going' (p. 6). The process requires both time and space in order to still ourselves from distractions and free ourselves from 'anxious thoughts and imaginings'.[2] The people of God therefore become conscious of the community in which they have immersed themselves.

The Eucharist is a celebratory feast, *eucharistia* meaning 'thanksgiving'. The eucharistic community gathers in the present moment to echo the words and actions which took place in that upper room in Jerusalem the night before Jesus died. The corporate body is made up of individuals, all with stories to tell which somehow connect with and relate to a common narrative which, told in the scriptures, is present in the sacrament. The Preparation–Gathering is a time of change, a transition point when a conscious choice is made – that is, to share one's personal story with God's story. It is at such times of transition that we make ourselves vulnerable and open to change. In a liturgical context, the worshipper gives up self-will and control, and becomes responsive to God's holy presence.

The importance of preparing well for a change, of gathering with others in order to be transformed by God, is paramount. When we prepare ourselves for the Eucharist we are asked to bring our whole selves to the altar of God – the place of sacrifice. We gather as broken pieces of Christ's body – God does not expect to meet us in our own strength. If we understand that, through the transformative sacramental nature of the Eucharist, we leave church in a different state from that in which we entered it, it is possible to understand why change need not be a negative state. When we put ourselves at God's mercy, surrendering ourselves to him, he meets us in our greatest need. Similarly, the Preparation–Gathering gives us opportunity to gather as broken people in need and in desire to enter a relationship of love.

A call to communion

My arrival at St Andrew's also represented a major time of transition for the parish. It had been ably served by its churchwardens and laity during the interregnum. The appointment of a new priest once more activated transition and change. I was also eager to make my mark and to establish my own ground rules which I wrote in the form of a vision statement for my first sermon. I have included it here in part:

> My vision is essentially a catholic creed, a song of the heart, and this is my song:
>
> - I believe in a church which discovers the untruth from within and exposes it to God's forgiveness.
> - I believe in a church which creates a sense of wonder and awe through its liturgy yet is not dour or regressive.
> - I believe in a church which encourages people, all of whom are made in the image of God, male and female, poor and rich, white and black, young and old.
> - I believe in a church which believes in resurrection, where conflicts are resolved and differences are accepted as a part of life.
> - I believe in a church whose members support each other, pray for each other, lay hands on each other and wash the feet of strangers at the door.

This statement of belief was written as an attempt to galvanize the community of faith. I wanted the community to consider its discipleship in terms of the penitential rite of preparation.

*   *   *

The story of John the Baptizer was for me a helpful spiritual resource because he is so representative of the rite of Preparation–Gathering. The Gospel of Mark gives a wonderful description of John, seemingly a rebel, an outcast, a danger to good society. John heeded the words of the prophet Isaiah, 'Make straight the way of the Lord' (Isaiah 40.3). John was given a commission by God to prepare the world for Jesus' ministry. As crowds gathered in the Judaean desert, John preached a revolutionary sermon: 'Repent.' What terrible and great disturbance erupted in the Judaean desert. Never had the world anticipated such closeness to God. Jesus, the Christ, was disturbed in mind and spirit and entered into this desert place in order for his ministry to be consecrated by his Father through baptism.

The wilderness was a place of amazing transition in the life of Jesus; it signalled his own public ministry. John was the first to witness Jesus' sacrificial journey between two locations of death: the Jordan desert and Calvary or Golgotha, the place of the skull. Madness and demons were associated with both places, yet here God insisted that the 'Good News' would be declared. The rite of Preparation–Gathering says a lot about the need to heed John's preaching: repent, ask for forgiveness, unburden your soul from the cares of this world. Such acts of penitence prepare the believer to meet truth and therefore the God of truth. This is the transition which prepares God's people to welcome the Lamb in the desert of repentance. The space given at the start of the liturgy is designed to be a desert space where we may struggle with the extremes of the desert heat – its isolation, its lack of nourishment, its dryness, its silence, its demons, madness and terror. A penitential heart is one that experiences these extremes that John the Baptist lived and preached. We gather and prepare in all eucharistic celebrations to meet the Lamb of God in all truth. He welcomes us despite ourselves. He welcomes who we are.

For me the penitential rite at the beginning of the Eucharist is a time of revelation, like the sun bursting to be dawned. I understand my own depression to have been a near-death experience. My desert was so arid that I could not see a way out of it. In such desperate times God never ceases to love. I also had the fellowship of John and a host of others who shouted in pain and anguish in their own wilderness places. Who knows where John the Baptist was on the mental health spectrum during his desert existence. Yet God chose John to baptize his own son. What folly, what madness, what love! I am grateful to God that living the Christ-life does not correspond to the world's definition of sanity. That is not to say that insanity is glorified in a Christian context but, as St Paul notes, 'For the message about the cross is foolishness' (1 Corinthians 1.18).

Restoring community

Let us return to our parish setting. This particular place of folly, like the Jordan valley and Golgotha, constituted a diverse mix of people. This was David's legacy – a parable of inclusion, fellowship and coexistence. It was also the focus of Jesus' short ministry, the replaying of Isaiah's prophecy 'to bring good news to the oppressed, to bind up the broken-hearted, to proclaim liberty to the captives, and release to the prisoners' (Isaiah 61.1).

We all depended upon God's transforming care. These people, broken and fragmented, wonderfully evoked the kingdom of God in its earthly incarnation. St Andrew's was a testimony to the everyday working out of God's kingdom in the here and now. It seemed at times quite 'unholy' but very real and very present. This eucharistic community was made up of individuals, all with stories to share, which somehow connected with and related to God's story of care and salvation.

The purpose of the Preparation–Gathering is to enable and empower the people to make the transition from telling their story to listening to God's story. The burden of sin and the denial and betrayal are taken from us. Now, with our senses alive to God's possibility, we hear the divinely inspired word.

We had all gathered to witness the start of a new ministry and a shared journey of faith. It was now imperative to understand and make understood what this meant in terms of the eucharistic rite and in terms of our lives in Christ who transforms all life. If we were to be changed, we were surely called to listen to the Christ that had called us together. The collected disturbance which the parish had suffered would necessarily continue as we listened to God's story and each other's stories.

Chapter 6

Psychological Assessment

The term 'assessment' is a clinical one. It speaks of a litany of questions and history-taking; of scribbled notes and standardized questionnaires. It fails, as a word, to go beyond this and conjure up what psychological assessment more fully entails: the coming together of two or more individuals, at least one professional and one lay; the opportunity to explore an individual's story and its meaning; to consider what it is that has brought them to this place and how they might journey on.

While psychological assessment is a secular process, for the purpose of this chapter I am keen to consider how central components of this process might have a bearing on the liturgy. In other words, how might psychological assessment inform our understanding of the preparation–gathering phase of the Eucharist? And what might this understanding tell us about preparing to respond to mental health issues in parish ministry?

The system (or 'gathering')

> For where two or three are gathered in my name, I am there among them. (Matthew 18.20)

As a clinical psychologist working in the NHS, it is not always possible to predict who might or might not be attending an initial assessment. The uncertainty of this is based on a number of factors: despite letters, even telephone calls in advance, individuals or families do not always confirm their attendance of an appointment and, even if they do, are not always clear about who they may or may not be bringing with them. At the most extreme end, I have expected a mother with her four-year-old boy, only to be greeted in the waiting-room by several siblings, an aunt and a grandmother. At the other end of the spectrum, when a colleague and I have invited a nuclear family to a family therapy session, we have found ourselves on a two-to-one with the father or mother – creating, therefore, the sometimes uncomfortable situation where the number of professionals outnumbers that of the client.

In a very different way, the gathering of the people for the Eucharist is equally unpredictable, if not more so. This unpredictability highlights the need for flexibility on the part of the priest as well as the people themselves. This flexibility might, though, run the risk of over-spilling if it were not for the boundaries inherent in the eucharistic service itself. The nature of these boundaries will be explored below. First, though, it is helpful to consider who and what comprises a 'gathering', and how we might understand this in psychological terms.

*   *   *

As individuals, we are all located within a system or systems that exist at different levels. This concept goes to the heart of systemic thinking, a key influence in clinical psychology. The 'Preparation–Gathering' phase of the Eucharist marks the coming together of a body of people who, for that hour of worship, signify a corporate whole. From a systemic perspective, this gathering (or congregation) represents a system of people that can be divided into smaller groups or systems (for example choir, altar party and welcome team). In my work, one way in which a system is illustrated is a family tree. When I meet with a family for the first time, a family tree can help provide a powerful illustration of the pattern of relationships within that family, including key events such as births, deaths and marriages. It can also locate a family within wider systems such as employment and educational bodies. For a priest, therefore, who is embarking on a new parish ministry, part of the 'assessment' process is also to try to understand the many systems and relationships that inform his new parish.

The institutions of the Anglican Church and the NHS were the two key systems which Gavin and I respectively inhabited during our time living and working in Fulham Fields. In systemic terms, Gavin's licensing to the parish of St Andrew's marked a significant shift in the already existing system and brought with it a new set of personal ideas and stories which in time he would share with the people of St Andrew's. There was, then, a critical transition period in which Gavin and his new flock got to know each other's concerns and stories – what it was that engaged them, mobilized them, or caused them to stand still.

The story

How I elicit and respond to a client's story is guided by one or more psychological models. How I enquire and think about an individual's psychological difficulties will depend on which model I am drawing from. Let us imagine for a moment a fictional character, Jane, who presents to her GP with a combination of depression and anxiety. I know from the referral that these difficulties are preventing her from leaving the house, from enjoying activities that she used to enjoy, and from sleeping at night. If working within the framework of cognitive behaviour therapy (CBT), I would wish to elicit a detailed picture of Jane's thoughts and feelings which relate to her difficulties: for example, 'Nobody likes me', 'I can't cope', 'I feel stupid and a burden to others'. This is because a key tenet of CBT is that an individual's behaviour is influenced by the way in which they respond to and interpret everyday situations (Kirk, 1998).

By contrast, if I wanted to engage with Jane's world from a perspective of 'brief solution-focused therapy', my line of questioning would take a different turn: 'The emphasis [would be] to move to a focus on solutions, rather than just the problems' (Dallos and Draper, 2005, p. 104). I would want to gain a detailed description not of the problems *per se* but of exceptions to the problems, of Jane's strengths, resources and coping strategies. As such, I might ask her to think of an occasion in the past week when she had felt able to leave the house, however briefly, despite her depression and anxiety. In this way I would seek to bring to her notice any positive changes she had already made; and these changes would then be used as building-blocks from which further change could occur (Dallos and Draper, 2005, p. 106).

These two examples of psychological assessment are less than snapshots. Hopefully, however, they do provide an insight into the types of models that can inform psychological thinking. The breadth and depth of these models stem from the richness and complexity of human stories, particularly where mental health plays a key part. It goes without saying that the ways in which we, as individuals within a parish community, be we lay or ordained, seek to find out and listen to others' stories, will clearly not be grounded in any theoretical approach. Perhaps, though, a more general lesson can be drawn from this: the importance of remembering that we all have stories to tell and stories to be listened to.

For St Andrew's, Fulham Fields, the dominant story that Gavin and I inherited was that of David's death. The tragic nature of this death meant that the congregation and parish as a whole had no opportunity to prepare for the end of their priest's ministry. When a traumatic event occurs, be this a bereavement, physical illness, divorce or other trauma, the rhythm of people's everyday lives and stories is interrupted in the most painful and unforeseen way. Depending on the context, this 'interruption' is likely to highlight pre-existing vulnerabilities and fragilities in individuals, in families and even in whole communities.

A parish assessment

When a priest is invited to take a look at a parish with a view to possibly becoming its next incumbent, some degree of 'assessment' necessarily takes place. A spouse's role in this process is a rather strange one – crucial, I suppose, yet necessarily subsidiary. When Gavin first told me about the prospect of St Andrew's, my immediate reaction (not one I am necessarily proud of), related to the vicarage. 'Sounds great,' I said, 'let's take a look – but of course we shan't live in the house.' I watched Gavin's face fall and knew from his expression that he had anticipated my response. 'Let's not pre-judge it, shall we?' 'Fine', I said, but inwardly I was determined.

On the day of the interview, we arranged to meet the area dean for lunch. He, warm and enthusiastic, provided us with an honest assessment of the parish and its people as he knew it. Clearly he had been involved during the course of a very difficult and unexpected interregnum and, as we talked, I felt a strange sense of bereavement – strange because it was not my bereavement. I had not known David, and yet, during these early conversations, I felt as though I were starting to gain a sense of him and the flock he had ministered to. I was very concerned about Gavin taking the place of someone so loved and so mourned by the people. I somehow felt part of the bereavement that the people had experienced, yet I was not part of it. I watched Gavin's face as we all spoke, and I knew that each of us was far from certain.

After lunch, we met with one of the churchwardens and in time she said she would show us around the vicarage. I was nervous, not least because I was aware that the house must be so familiar to her; clearly she had spent many happy hours there. I felt we were encroaching on others' territory and that really we should stay away. What was more, I felt at a loss how to react when looking around. We were shown through the front door into the hallway and we all commented on the tiles. Such a banal comment, it seemed in the circumstances, and yet it was true: the tiles were the first feature I was drawn to. That said, I did not feel disposed to concentrate on the house. There seemed little point when I had no intention of living there.

The house had a new front door and was empty. Of course it was empty, but somehow this struck me more than anything else. It seemed so quiet, so terribly quiet and still. Everything that had been had gone; all, that is, save a few books and an old bookcase in David's study. I did not know which I found hardest – its crude emptiness or the few material reminders of David that still existed. These reminders, though, belonged to the study only. The rest had all been uprooted – ripped out, it seemed to me. There were no curtains, no carpets, no curtain rails even. Everything had been painted white. Even the windows had been whitewashed for forensic reasons following David's murder. There seemed nothing left except the former shell that once had been. Nothing left and nothing I could connect with. The house was somehow symbolic of my own fears and my own difficulties of crossing an unknown threshold. As such, it repeated my feelings expressed in the frontispiece of this book: *I am not here, I have not visited this place, tell no one.*

The floorboards echoed beneath our feet. As they did so, they seemed to call out to my own contradictory voices which I sought to repress: on the one hand, hollow and empty, asking me to stay away; on the other, filled with a rich resonance I could not ignore – inviting me, teasing me even to listen and respond. They had many terrains, many voices and many magnitudes.

We had reached the middle landing. Gavin was ahead of me and I heard him comment on the skylight. I looked up. I had not noticed it previously. It was, I had to admit, a fine feature. It furnished the stairs and landing with a shaft of light and I continued climbing. It offered the possibility of refreshment on dark, gloomy days and I could not help but admire it. I hesitated and, in those first moments of hesitation, I started to conceive new possibilities. Afraid of my own ambivalence, afraid lest it should cause me to do something against my will, I turned my eye instead to the dust and cracks that the light exposed.

But I was too late. A seed had already been planted that perhaps I had entered a place that was akin to me after all. This innocuous, almost neutral space, caught part in shadow, part by the light, was not what I had imagined. It was perhaps as the house had always been. It was where I wanted the house to return to. It was the part that had best survived and which spoke to me. It was here that I started to understand that, if Gavin were to be incumbent of this parish, perhaps we would live in the house after all. But we would have to invite the parish back in so they could realize it for themselves. This, I came to understand, would be key to our preparation.

Establishing boundaries

As a trainee clinical psychologist, I was necessarily conscientious about the way in which I prepared myself for meeting with a client for the first time. I would take time to read the file in detail; then, depending on what information was available, I would take what I had learned to supervision and discuss the referral with my supervisor. Together we would consider possible areas I might explore at the initial meeting and what hypotheses the referral seemed to raise.

This kind of preparation was not about pre-empting an individual's story, unique to them, even before meeting them. It was, however, about carving out the time and space to be curious about a client's story; to generate hypotheses in a way which enabled me to think creatively when I met with them in person. When I failed to give myself (and my client) this time, I was in danger of preventing this space to listen and reflect in the sessions themselves. The role of preparation is, therefore, invaluable, and it is with a degree of shame that I confess that this time spent preparing for clinical sessions was one of the first things to go once I qualified. As time progressed and my case load increased, I often struggled to snatch a few minutes, sometimes moments, to prepare for a session with a client. Furthermore, this preparation time was most at risk when I let other core areas of my professional life slip: namely, regular supervision, professional peer support, access to ongoing training, and personal reading. These are, in many ways, my foundation blocks, essential to good practice. Without them, I flounder.

In the years I have known Gavin, it has struck me that a priest has similar challenges; and that these challenges come to a head, just as they did with me when I qualified, in the transition phases from ordinand to curate and, most pertinently, from curate to incumbent. As other factors compete with a parish priest's time – boilers, committees, church buildings and struggling finances – the discipline of his own prayer life and even the daily offices themselves are quickly under siege. This highlights the obvious importance for a priest's own structures about which I am poorly qualified to speak, but which include spiritual direction, cell groups, training opportunities, personal reading, prayer time and quiet time. These structures were every bit as important for Gavin in his work, if not more, as the equivalent structures were for me in mine. When he let these slip, his personal and professional boundaries were both put to the test in one measure.

*   *   *

Ensuring the boundaries of our professional and personal lives is no easy task. As a clinical psychologist, the extent to which I am prepared for an assessment (or indeed any subsequent session) is not confined to reading and considering the client's file in advance. My readiness to listen and hear each story afresh is also rooted in several practical considerations. Have I booked a room in advance or am I scrabbling around for one at the last minute? Am I on time or have I over-stretched myself, become side-tracked on the telephone before rushing over to the waiting-room when the client arrives? Assuming I have booked a room, have I prepared it appropriately – are there enough chairs; are toys laid out if necessary; have I removed all signs from any client who has attended there before? Getting these things right are all initial steps in creating a safe environment for the client to tell and explore his or her story.

These practical steps have, therefore, important clinical implications. They help establish clear boundaries around a session. The concept of boundaries is complex and raises many questions which, in my work, I am required to remain alive and attentive to. As always, there are no hard and fast rules to these questions, but it is essential the questions are asked and given real consideration. Questions I might ask myself, then, when setting up an initial assessment are: Do I telephone or write to the client? If so, do I do so in person or do I ask our team secretary to act on my behalf? Do I arrange to see the client in the same room at the same time on each occasion, or do the constraints of the building I am working in and my own work schedule not allow this? If these are not options, should I somehow make it work? How long should sessions last and with what frequency? In reflecting on these apparently mundane issues, I am seeking to explore how the parameters of time and space will impact on the boundaries of my relationship with a client.

This kind of reflection had equal bearing on our time at St Andrew's. When we first moved into the vicarage, we already had various preconceived ideas about the boundaries of our new home. In practical terms, this meant that parish life was confined to downstairs where we had a hallway, the lounge/dining room, Gavin's study, the kitchen and a toilet. Parish and family life clearly overlapped at times. In many ways I missed these overlaps when we left St Andrew's. They were part of the rich tapestry of parish living which perhaps I did not fully appreciate until I had left it. At the same time, by giving ourselves an additional 'upstairs living-room' and keeping the ground and first floors separate, family life also had the option of privacy when needed. This need for separateness went, of course, two ways. It was often not appropriate for me to be present when Gavin had parishioners visit – pastoral work, in particular, brought with it strong issues of confidentiality.

The second 'ground rule' we established in our minds, and which was particularly important for me, was not to allow into the house anybody we did not know. This concern on my part was in many ways a direct consequence of David's death. It was also, however, a response to David's own style of ministry. David had had a very 'open door' policy during his time at St Andrew's. His welcome to all people literally took all people over his threshold at all hours. Gavin and I were anxious to establish a new set of boundaries in the house which we hoped would work for us. This was partly a consequence of our concerns about safety following David's murder but also reflected something of our own ethos for parish ministry. Our ideas about boundaries were, however, constantly being tested and put under review when we first moved into the vicarage.

It is one thing establishing a rule in your head; it is another putting that rule into practice. We had been in the vicarage a matter of days. Gavin and I were in the back garden. The doorbell rang and I went inside to answer it. At the door was a woman, probably about my age, with bruises on her face. She said she had been beaten up; she had no money, and needed money for the electricity meter for her children. I let her in. Having done so, I realized I was uncomfortable and at a loss as to how to behave. On the one hand I felt a wretchedness and empathy, combined with feelings of guilt, for my visitor. On the other I felt I was being put upon; I had a growing instinct that her story was not the full story, and I berated myself both for my possible naivety and for what could be deemed my judgemental attitude.

I am not sure why, but I let her into Gavin's study. As this was by no means a neutral space, this was probably the last thing I should have done. I then went into the garden to fetch Gavin. He came through quickly and, after a short deliberation, he gave her food instead of money and she soon left us. Over the next months we had many such visits and never really reached a clear conclusion about how to manage these cries for help. I became better at not letting people over the threshold, particularly when on my own, and I familiarized myself with some local agencies and shelters which could offer support. Perhaps, though, one crucial error I made in this first instance was not to pause when listening to the woman's story; to pause and understand that I could listen and respond to her story without transgressing my own fragile boundaries of space.

From a lay perspective, the eucharistic service provides a powerful metaphor for safe and boundaried space. It happens at the same time in the same place each week; its length is by and large predictable. Regardless of who turns up, or at whatever stage in the service, the service will take place. The priest is constant and can be relied upon to celebrate at that time. What is more, the actual process of getting ready for a service involves several practical procedures. During our three years at St Andrew's I quite often used to join Gavin and his faithful sacristan before the Tuesday evening Eucharist. As I watched them prepare for this service, I used to take still comfort from the sacred space they moved about in – altering cloths, laying out service sheets, preparing bread and wine, moving chairs if necessary. All this felt like a symbolic reminder of the importance of getting ready.

Getting ready

Gavin and I took the matter of preparing for life at St Andrew's very seriously. At a practical level this involved several painting days in the vicarage just before moving in. Room by room, we slowly painted the house. As we did so, the floorboards that had previously haunted me would continue to echo, but their echoes now would be vibrant. My brother, a classical guitarist, would often join us to practise while we painted. The music would fill the house. On late-spring evenings the sound would carry through the house and we would all be filled with a great sense of purpose.

Our relationship to the vicarage in many ways acted as a symbolic transition point between David's ministry and our new beginning. Just before the furniture moved in, Gavin and I invited the PCC round for drinks. It was a fine summer's evening. The members arrived in dribs and drabs. Many came in small groups, bringing with them a whole host of gifts and vulnerabilities, visible and invisible: laughter, humility, warmth, a great sense of dress, West Indian cooking and humour, loss of sight, partial hearing, eccentricities, foibles, anxieties, hope, a love of music – the qualities were many and varied, but common to them all was a huge welcome. Other qualities, including some difficulties, would emerge over time, but on this night how welcomed we felt and how happy we were to open up the house to our new brethren.

On that first occasion, as the house was not yet furnished, we put aside the boundaries we would later adopt and threw open the whole house. PCC members, occasional spouse, children, all wandered freely. Given the very difficult, understandable feelings that had become connected with the house since David's death (many had not wanted to go into it), a pre-emptive housewarming seemed important. Wine glasses visited the bedrooms, the landings, the upstairs living-room, the attic rooms, the cupboards (where the children hid) and the bathrooms.

The drinks party marked the happy end of an already long day. As we came to leave, we hardly noticed a fellow neighbour appear from one of the flats opposite. Awoken from our domestic chat, it must have seemed as though we appeared from the shadows. The man – Clive, we learned – crossed over to greet us. He explained he had been out all day and, having just got back, it was a shock to see people in the house. He spoke of how the house had been locked up for 18 months and how pleased he was to see it inhabited again. Nonetheless he had not expected anyone just yet. We explained we would be moving in shortly, and said we were greatly looking forward to it.

Clive was warm and welcoming. Again and again he repeated how pleased they would be to see the house lived in once more. We spoke briefly of David's death, and of how it had affected not just David's congregation but the whole parish. The conversation left me excited but daunted. This brief encounter renewed my sense of the task ahead. The area dean had named this task a while previously: 'You will heal that house', he had said. At the time I had shrunk from his words, and now I was starting to understand why. A bit like Clive: on the one hand, still conscious of the past, on the other, crying out for a new beginning, I too was fearful of and drawn to the expectations that may or may not await us. The multiple layers of the story we were about to enter – that utterly human yet Christ-embodied task of 'healing' – was only now upon me.

Integrating Mind and Spirit (Part 3)

Starting out

Starting out in a parish requires an honest assessment not only of the people and place but of oneself. This desire to be open to God's truth helps facilitate an awareness and understanding of the parish and its people. Discerning conflict, division, unhappiness and struggling health is the task of confession. It also goes to the heart of psychological assessment. For the parish priest, this task is extended beyond the boundaries of a liturgical setting to the everyday of his parishioners' lives.

Listening to other people's stories of loss, trauma and mental health breakdown can be painful, at times overwhelming. It is essential, therefore, that a parish priest feels equipped to respond to mental health problems in a way which offers some degree of containment. To do this, he cannot be a quasi mental health practitioner. He can, however, seek to be in a place which best prepares him for responding sensitively to mental health issues. The aim is to reflect something of the unconditional regard held by God for all of his people.

Practical implications

It would be irresponsible for this book to suggest that there is a clear set of guidelines that a priest can follow to help ascertain mental health problems. Here, though, are some pointers which may be helpful to hold in mind (adapted from Lindsay and Powell, 1994):

- Why has the individual approached you now?
- How far back do the difficulties date?

- What is the individual's situation (e.g. married, children, single, homeless, employed, unemployed etc.)?
- In what ways are the problems impacting on the individual's life (e.g. family, working relationships, sleep and eating patterns)?
- How is the individual coping with the problem (e.g. drug, alcohol use; anti-depressants)?
- What thoughts are occupying or troubling the individual most? To what extent are these thoughts intruding on his or her daily living?
- How is the individual interpreting events? For example, does he or she seem to hold any abnormal or paranoid beliefs about how others think about or behave towards himself or herself? Does the individual's beliefs about his or her body size or image seem unfounded? Does the individual have particularly low self-worth or fears of not coping which appear disproportionate to the situation?
- Is the individual experiencing any auditory hallucinations (i.e. hearing voices) or visual hallucinations or sensory abnormalities (e.g. feelings of numbness or tingling sensations in extremities)?
- Are there striking features about the individual's appearance and behaviour: e.g. unusual movements or posture, speech abnormalities (either very loud or quiet, too fast or too slow, constantly interrupting)?
- How does the individual perceive his or her difficulties, e.g. does he or she perceive them as inconsequential or endangering their wellbeing?
- Who is supporting the individual, if at all? What previous or current help has the individual received or are they receiving from other professionals (e.g. psychiatry, psychology, GP)? (See below.)

Though a priest may feel out of his depth regarding mental health issues, his rootedness in liturgy should in fact set him up in order to understand something of the importance of being prepared to engage with others.

A priest's sacramental role enables him to reconcile people with God to absolve them of their past regrets and burdens. The penitential rite therefore prepares both priest and people to be ready to hear God's word in a safe and boundaried context. This process which aids listening, safety and containment needs somehow to be translated onto all other pastoral encounters:

- Listening and readiness to listen are key skills in any pastoral encounter, planned or spontaneous. In order to listen and listen well, a priest is required to put to one side his own distractions, and be attentive and willing to hear what is being said. Listening needs to be non-judgemental while at the same time maintaining the listener's own integrity. The rhythm of a priest's life with its daily offices helps keep him in a good emotional and spiritual place in which to do this.
- Establishing a relationship with somebody with mental health difficulties brings with it considerable responsibility – the need for empathy, respect and consistency as well as a realistic assessment of one's own limitations in that relationship.
- By finding out what support systems are already in place for an individual with mental health difficulties (for example friends, family, parishioners, professionals), the priest is able to locate himself in a wider systemic network of support.
- When establishing boundaries around a pastoral encounter, flexibility and discernment are needed. Factors to consider in any pastoral encounter include:
  - the way in which we relate to somebody else given the context: for example our tone of voice, use of humour, degree of familiarity;
  - time: for example, punctuality, putting a time-limit on meetings;
  - place: for example, give consideration to where the meeting takes place, public or private (consider having a colleague present in some situations), who knows it is taking place, seeking thereby to safeguard both priest and parishioner.
- When establishing boundaries within the vicarage, each priest needs to work out for himself (incorporating family life if that is applicable) what works for him. Some boundaries which might be helpful are:
  - being clear with parishioners about time off and sticking to it;
  - a separate living space;
  - separate telephone lines;
  - a clear demarcation between certain family and parish responsibilities.
- When setting up safety procedures with priest and/or parishioners in mind, these need to relate to both the church and the vicarage. For a fuller discussion, see National Churchwatch (cited in the Bibliography), but guidelines include:

- closing the church at night;
- suitable lighting around the church;
- CCTV;
- secure locks;
- a spy-hole in the vicarage front door;
- preparation for the unexpected (e.g. late-night visit) – familiarizing oneself with local resources, for example mental health charities, counselling services and night shelters, etc.

Questions for individual reflection and/or discussion

1. How as an individual do you feel you prepare for worship? How might this inform your preparation for other encounters in parish life?
2. How difficult is it to get alongside those who suffer from mental health problems? What voice does mental health have in your church?
3. Consider the different roles and structures within your parish community. In what ways do these help and support those with mental health difficulties?
4. (a) Which boundaries do you feel helpfully inform your parish ministry? Are there any areas you would like to change?
   (b) What safety structures has your church already put in place? In what ways might you improve these further?

A prayer of confession

God of mercy,
at times our burdens overcome us
and darkness overshadows our trust in you.
Forgive our unbelief.
Do not leave our presence but draw us to yourself,
that we may live in you as you live in us.
Renew our spirit and kindle the flame of love,
for your kingdom's coming.
Amen.

Part 4

Listening and Meaning

The following two chapters explore how our attention to and interpretation of stories can inform our understanding of mental health in parish life.

The Liturgy of the Word dramatizes the holy scriptures in a body of writings which might disturb both mind and spirit through individual stories of brokenness, transformation and healing. We are invited not only to listen to these stories but to engage more deeply with their multiple layers of meaning. The invitation to hear and interpret the holy scriptures is then transposed onto the context of parish life.

The process of psychological formulation refers to the way in which we try to understand and interpret an individual's difficulties, drawing on a range of models and theories. The broad and dynamic nature of this approach resonates strongly with the process of story-telling and story-listening in a liturgical context. As with our responses to the holy scriptures, our psychological understanding of individuals' stories is constantly being tested and reinterpreted as new information and new possibilities come to light.

Chapter 7

The Liturgy of the Word

A book of disturbance

The Bible is a book of disturbance. Throughout its history, the holy scriptures have told the story of desire, pain, loss, joy and hope. The writers of the word of God were, we understand, divinely inspired. They told the story of God through revelation and their own limitation. This is why scripture is so profoundly human, so utterly earthed and rooted. Without understanding these key characteristics in the authorship of the Bible, the modern-day reader is unable to grasp the full significance of the writing. The land of the ancient Near East did not understand what mental health was, nor did the first-century Palestinians during Jesus' ministry.

The Old Testament disturbs the people of God to believe in the one, true God and gathers this believing community into a promised place. The story of the 'great family', of Abraham and Sarah, encapsulates the emotional landscape of all of God's people and how this disturbance of mind and spirit is rooted in the human condition:

> One night God brought Abram outside. He looked up into the sky. God came so close to Abram and Abram came so close to God, that Abram knew what God was saying. 'You will become the father of a great family, and Sarai will be the mother. The members of the great family will be as many as there are stars in the sky and grains of sand in the desert.' Abram laughed. (Berryman, 2002, p. 62)

The psalms within the Old Testament describe various levels of disturbance, most notably anger, praise and lament. The psalms were written to be sung and shared. They contained within them the history of the Jewish people. Many of the psalms were attributed to David, the shepherd boy, turned mighty warrior, turned celebrated king. The narrative of the Jews continues afresh in the New Testament writings. The subject remains the same – God's love for his people. The New Testament reveals the disturbing and hope-filled prophecy of the Old by fulfilling God's promise of salvation in a form and nature that few would recognize in the Gospels. Echoing the essence of the Preparation–Gathering chapter, Walker (1996) describes the word of God as the continuation of our personal journey into God's story: 'For there is a story, once widely known, that tells us who we are, where we came from, and where we are going . . . This story is told by Christians and it is called the gospel' (p. 2). The remainder of the New Testament portrays the growth of the early Church in its struggle to survive against persecutory forces.

This sweep of human and divine history lived and breathed throughout four millennia of story-telling ultimately presents a narrative of passion – the love of God for his people and the difficulty that these people experience in living this gift of love. This story, then, runs through the heart of Christian communities to this very day. The Liturgy of the Word is not, however, solely limited to story-telling, important as that is. This is the rite of understanding, of overlaying the rich textures of faith and belief upon the pattern of our own lives today.

The process of interpretation starts with the prayer that literally 'collects' all our thoughts. It is encouraged through the sermon or homily; it is prompted and prodded through the corporate declaration of faith in the creeds; and finally it is offered back to God through the intercessions. This process is not set in stone. As Countryman (2001) writes: 'The Bible is not a book that answers all questions. It is a book that keeps inspiring new questions, new insights, new conversion and change of heart in us' (p. 43). The significance of God's word and his relationship with the people of St Andrew's, Fulham Fields, was in part a story of disturbance of mind and spirit. I will, in this chapter, try to elucidate how the Liturgy of the Word might be able to aid our understanding that wholeness among brokenness is the triumph of our faith.

The encounter of God's story and our story

The Liturgy of the Word is very much a dialogue between the word that is God and the one made in God's image: 'From the waters of chaos you drew forth the world, and in your great love, fashioned us in your image' (*Celebrating Common Prayer*, 1992, p. 13).

Chaos seemed to rule Jad's life. He started to come to church during my ministry at St Andrew's. I cannot remember when he first made an appearance but he quickly became a loved member of the community of faith. His testimony brought me closer to understanding the nature of God. In truth, Jad's story tells me something of God's story. I am better able to know God for knowing Jad.

Jad's history was somewhat confusing. He was a political refugee who had settled in London a decade or so before. His experiences in his homeland had wounded him painfully. If anybody in church referred to his country of origin, he would leave the service and not return for a week or so. He frequently arrived late to church, often in an agitated state. On these occasions his prayers were frequently audible, interrupting the flow of the liturgy. He would stand to one side for the distribution of the sacrament and offer his cap before receiving the host. This ritual happened each time God's people assembled to share at the Lord's table at St Andrew's. Jad's story of disturbance was one of many.

Hans had been a regular at St Andrew's for many years and was a very faithful worshipper. He had a history of mental ill health which caused great concern to his family. He was a private person, not wanting to cause a fuss, determined to disguise that which held him captive. I had to be careful not to overload Hans with church tasks and responsibilities, worrying that these pressures would cause more harm than good. He suffered a particularly chronic episode of depression and was admitted to hospital. He spent some time there sectioned for his own safety. I remember an occasion when visiting him during this period when Hans wanted me to help make sense of his experiences. He was concerned that the caring God that he had believed in for so long was in fact deserting him. Our conversation then and our future dialogue centred on the possibility that God is present in all of us, accompanying us even in our moments of greatest fear. Hans understood at some level that I was not discrediting his very real fear of abandonment, but that the story of Jesus is the story of irrefutable and boundless love.

The third person I want to introduce whose story reflects something of the beauty of the parishioners that I grew to love involves Annette. She was a very nervous lady whose husband had died two years previously and left her very isolated. Her timidity was indicative of a more wide-spread anxiety which was present throughout the parish. I would encounter Annette venturing into the church, to light a candle. She was quite afraid of life and people. She rarely came to the Eucharist; when she did, it was a triumph of her resolve against all the forces which enrolled against her. Emotion was never far from her face. She cried when she was offered kindness, and knitted hats and gloves for the youngest members of the congregation, generous symbols of her appreciation of the friendship offered to her. This is a short extract from a life which again encounters and yields the mystery of love.

The parish of Fulham Fields is composed of many such stories, many images which are marked by the world and anointed by God. They communicate God's divine plan that Christ is at the heart of who we are as people. Jad, Hans and Annette all proclaim the message of incarnation – God with us in body, mind and spirit. I cannot help but know that Christ is alive in the loss, pain, fear and transcendent beauty of Jad, Hans and Annette. God's story and our own stories become mutually dependent when we use the language of faith. Jad, Hans and Annette were all able to share a divine narrative and use it to cling on dearly to some sense of worth. For them it is surely a story of salvation, allowing them the freedom that they have in Christ to encounter God. Let us then examine God's story of the Word made flesh and see how God encounters all of us who are disturbed in mind and spirit.

*   *   *

The mystical sense of the prologue of the fourth Gospel, the Gospel according to St John, puts Jesus into context for us. Unlike the authors of the synoptic Gospels, John's Jesus was created before the world began. This was and is God's Word, not of our time but of God's eternity, not of our choosing but of God's love for his people:

> . . . in the beginning was the Word, the Word was, says the Greek, in relation to God 'pros ton theon', 'close to', 'with', yes, but most technically, 'in relationship to God'. So that the very first statement of St

John's gospel tells us that before anything else, there exists relationship . . . (Rowan Williams, 2006)

It is this gift of God's loving relationship which speaks most authentically to me about the story of Fulham Fields. The fragile elements of the congregation were somehow further enhanced by the church building of St Andrew's. The building, like many of its time and type, is a monument to Victorian heroism and optimism. It was built during the rapid enlargement of the area in the late nineteenth century. A watercolour sketch of the proposed church illustrates this Victorian edifice surrounded by fields and green spaces. It is a picture of a church in rude health, proud, responsible, a landmark in the life of the community.

The relationship that the church has enjoyed with its people and environs has changed radically. St Andrew's is now constrained within the limitations of an overcrowded city. Residential development has all but denied the church the sanctity of space. More than 100 years of urban life has ingrained itself upon the building's exterior. Inside, years of neglect, vandalism and theft have robbed the church of its former dignity and pride. The church was not watertight, the spire had sections of masonry missing and the brick needed re-pointing and replacing in certain areas. The windows were either smashed through vandalism or cracked by frost. The darker recesses of the church offered sanctuary to those agitated by others or themselves, who took respite in drink, drugs or harm. These stories of neglect, vandalism and theft go some way to tell the story of the sacred stones of the church and locate the story of the sacred people of the Church.

At a symbolic level, these stories describe something of the relationship between God and his people. John's Gospel 'dares to claim that [God] becomes flesh' (King, 2004). The Word literally pitched his tent among us. In other words, God becomes part of our everyday and of the life of everybody. Jerome Berryman describes this universal declaration of acceptance through the story of Abraham: 'there was one family that believed that all of God was in every place. They did not yet know that, but that is what they thought' (Berryman, 2002, p. 60). Such unconditional regard seems revelatory to a sometimes fragile and vulnerable listener of the word, possibly even unbelievable. Could we dare to believe in the midst of all that life presents that God not only relates to our story, but that he owns it?

This was a message that needed to be proclaimed in the traumatized streets of Fulham Fields. The inner urban chaos that at times character- ized this parish was not excluded from God's presence:

> . . . in order that we should understand the down-to-earth seriousness and life-transforming experience of the story, we find that the New Testament often talks of the gospel as something which needs to be 'announced' (*anagello*) or 'proclaimed' (*kerygma*). (Walker, 1996, p. 17)

So, what was the word of God proclaiming about the serious nature of trauma, grief and loss and all the component parts that make or break our mental health? This was obviously a community that desired to travel with God and seek his promise despite awful setbacks. This was a community that displayed enormous resilience and fortitude. The church not only celebrated Christ's paschal mystery with great sincerity, but it lived its own Easter experience too.

Living the Paschal mystery

St Andrew's experience of Easter raised particular questions for the com- munity because of its own story of loss and renewal. Could the Word made flesh be present in the disturbance of mind and spirit? If so, was God incarnate relating, sharing and communicating his love through our precious mental health? These questions remained largely unresolved during my incumbency. How difficult it was to reflect upon the benefits of this 'life-transforming' story within the lives of those who suffered terribly from the burden of their mental ill health. I had cause to visit the mental health unit at the neighbouring hospital on many occasions. Wearing a clerical suit and collar, I became used to being accosted by patients whose illusory fears voiced passion and mistrust. The Church represented for many a target for resentment, even abuse. The Church representative was therefore targeted by those who suffered from mania and delusion. These were for me deeply uncomfortable encounters. I was aware that there was a void of expectation in these dialogues that I could not satisfy. I did not understand their suffering. I only knew that their behaviour was at best irrational and at worst dangerous; most significantly a danger to themselves.

When my own parishioners were the cause of my visits to the local mental health unit, any learned applied theology or pastoral guidance quickly evaporated into the ether. My only real response was to locate myself physically at the point of need. Of course I would be there in kindness and gentleness, but the measure of my pastoral effort would be unaccountable, presumably hopeless. When encountering extreme pyschoses my pastoral response was severely limited. I hankered for help, guidance and expertise. Sometimes professional help was at hand, at other times I felt isolated and alone. Increasingly I became aware of my role as a carer in the community and the immense task that this role represented. The Church was rightly proud of its claim to be a sponsor of care professionals who lived and worked in the places of greatest social, economic and spiritual need. As my encounters with those suffering from mental ill health became more numerous, the wider my eyes were opened to such disturbances. These encounters took place in all areas of parish life – shops, offices, the streets, the church and the vicarage. Brokenness was a key aspect of those who chose to gather at St Andrew's and rely on the church's care as part of their *modus vivendi*.

Yet this was the precious gift of the St Andrew's community. It was due to their openness and part fragility, their great sense of fellowship and friendship, that they welcomed people in spite of who they were. Many were not 'churched', they did not necessarily behave in a way that was expected or 'normal'. This led to some anxiety whenever unsuspecting newcomers arrived. I had a concern that the growth of the church might be restricted by the brokenness of the place and the people. My brief was to try and encourage the growth of the church community in a way that would better reflect the demographics of the parish. The parish of St Andrew's was certainly a people of variety, comprising one-third Afro-Caribbean, one-third working-class Fulham families, and one-third aspirational city workers who were constantly moving in and out of the parish. Many of this last group preferred the more stable and refined places of worship which could offer something which St Andrew's was not.

The congregation at St Andrew's was growing though. Relationships were being strengthened, and trust, most importantly, was slowly being granted. I felt that God was communicating himself to us. The St Andrew's story of God incarnating himself, with tent and all, into the darker recesses of the place and the people, was evident. The Christ of the cross was present within the grief of David's murder and the awful isolation which visited the church community. But the story of the Word is that God brings his people back to himself. The miracle of Jesus' healings is that he brought those who were ostracized back into the fellowship of love.

Signs of the kingdom

God's story of relationships made whole through the Gospel narratives gives a different interpretation to the perspective of mental health. The Word made flesh cannot resist offering peace for his people, not least for those suffering from appalling psychoses, for example the Gerasene demoniac.

The story of the Gerasene demoniac, told by all three synoptic Gospel writers, may enlighten our sometimes fearful concern about mental illness. St Mark covers the story in most depth (Mark 5.1–20). He describes a tortured man, believed to be possessed by demons, who is forced to make the tombs his place of residence. The man must have been reviled and feared by the people of Gerasa as he was chained by them in what was for the Jews the most impure of places: 'Night and day among the tombs and on the mountains he was always howling and bruising himself with stones' (Mark 5.5). This man had been made an outcast, rejected by society and religion.

The story of the word is that God desires to repair the fractures of this man's disturbance. Jesus does not attempt to do anything without power, authority and love. It is through the use of these divine agents that Jesus is able to heal the man in the most dramatic of forms. But the healing continues after the 'demons' have been released. The healing concerns the repatriation of the man into the community. How will he be accepted? How will he forgive? What latent fears remain? In terms of God's mercy the message is clear – acceptance is possible if we love the whole person. In our ministry of healing, we are called not to 'rescue', but to allow the word to communicate in us and relate through us as it removes personal prejudice and anxiety.

During my vocational journey I have had course throughout theological training, curacy and incumbency to visit places which, through my uncertain eyes, have reflected aspects of the landscape of Gerasa. On such visits – for example, to mental health in-patient units, nursing homes, community halls, schools and private dwellings – I have witnessed incidents of isolation, ostracism and fear. These have emotional responses to the 'demons' which, in modern-day thinking, we might describe as disturbance or difference, responses which have led us to chain and shackle, even incarcerate those we find difficult to relate to.

As my ministry has progressed, however, these painful experiences of care have been put into perspective by the many and various examples of compassion and healing which serve as signs of the kingdom today. St Andrew's, for example, was a church community which tried to counter the fearful culture of the age by demonstrating that difference is an integrity that belongs within the Church. By continuing Jesus' teaching and embodying his compassion and care, St Andrew's displayed continued signs of God's kingdom. The Word being made flesh was born again through the actions of God's people.

The premise that formulates this chapter is that the Bible is a book of disturbance. This disturbance not only tells the story of difference through the people of God but it also disturbs our understanding of how we might welcome and include people of difference. The Word inspires us to undertake the works of God – miraculous works. I understand that it was a miracle for Jad, Hans and Annette to enter the doors of the sacred space called St Andrew's. They were living the truth that, through our brokenness, together we may reveal a unity that is God. St Andrew's was a place of great humility which of course was also its strength. It offered an uncompromising 'Yes' to all who were sad and afraid. The Word was being heard, but in a surprising and altogether different way than I had ever expected. God was working his purpose out.

During the eucharistic feast, St Andrew's at times felt like the tent of meeting where holiness dwelt. Those who had helped pitch the tent alongside the Word suffered from the full variety of demons. They were legion: schizophrenia, bi-polar disorder, agoraphobia, anxiety, depression . . . the list goes on. This was our story. It was visible, for all to see. It was loud, for all to hear. It was reality, for all to understand. This is where God had made it known that his Son was to share his life in all of its fullness with all people.

Chapter 8

Psychological Formulation

Understanding stories

When we enter into relationship with one another, we ideally enter into a dialogue which seeks to understand one another's stories. In psychological terms, this search for meaning involves the generation and testing of hypotheses. Hypotheses are not idle reflections of a practitioner's imagination but are rooted in theory and practice. This process is known as 'formulation'.

While different psychological models may vary in how they think about and use the formulation process (Dallos and Draper, 2005, p. 151), the common theme of exploring and generating meaning prevails. Evolving patterns of understanding and interpretation are constantly being tested and retested as new information, new stories and new perspectives come to light. In this way, psychological formulation seems to reflect something of the dynamism of the Liturgy of the Word. To pick up on Gavin's earlier citation: 'The Bible is not a book that answers all questions [but one] that keeps inspiring new questions, new insights, new conversion and change of heart in us' (Countryman, 2001, p. 7). It is this same potential for asking again, seeing again, being changed again which, for me, goes to the heart of parish ministry.

The way in which we as individuals respond to and interpret the Bible is dependent on a variety of factors. These include our own level of knowledge of the Bible; the way in which we 'receive' the text on a given day, probably influenced by what is going on in our lives; our own stage of spiritual development; and our own style of churchmanship. Similarly, as a clinical psychologist, the way in which I think and enquire about an individual's story is affected by several biases: my level of experience, my own particular areas of expertise, the reliability of the information being presented to me, and my own theoretical orientation. The fact that my thinking and ideas are grounded in theory and research is central to a clinician's practice. This is one of the defining strengths of clinical psychology. To a much greater and more profound degree, so too the Liturgy of the Word (and, even more specifically, the Bible) is what roots the story of Christianity in a lasting framework.

Understanding stories of mental health and trauma

The biopsychosocial (BPS) model is one broad approach which can offer a useful way of thinking about mental health. While it was originally applied to the physiological condition of heart disease by the cardiologist George Engel (1977, cited by Gilbert, 2002), in more recent years the model has been applied to the context of mental health difficulties (see Kiesler, 1999, for a review, cited by Gilbert, 2002). From a BPS perspective, the degree to which we are vulnerable to experiencing mental health problems is dependent on three factors: biological (that is, our genetic predisposition to mental health problems); psychological (the cognitive processes which underpin our thoughts, behaviour and emotions); and social (influences in our social environment and relationships). These factors clearly all interrelate and are unique to each and every one of us.

The BPS model facilitates, therefore, thinking at a variety of levels. Individual differences, cognitions and events do not exist in isolation but form a complex system of interactions. External events such as a bereavement or trauma will inevitably affect each and every individual attached to that event in different ways. The notion is supported by the cognitive behavioural literature on post-traumatic stress syndrome (PTSD) which places particular emphasis on how individuals differ in their appraisal of trauma and its aftermath. In general terms, the model argues that the way in which an individual appraises a traumatic event contributes to the persistence (or subsidence) of PTSD symptoms (Ehlers and Clark, 2000). In other words, the way in which an individual processes and understands his personal story is seen as pivotal to his psychological recovery.

Cognitive behaviour therapy is not the only model which has applied itself to the psychological effects of trauma on individuals. From a psychoanalytical perspective:

> Trauma is a kind of wound. When we call an event *traumatic,* we are
> borrowing the word from the Greek where it refers to a piercing of the
> skin . . . Freud (1920) used the word metaphorically to emphasize how
> the mind too can be pierced and wounded by events . . . (Garland,
> 1998b, p. 9)

This perspective returns us to the story of St Andrew's, Fulham Fields.
For this parish, the trauma of David's death did not simply pierce 'one
mind'. It pierced an entire community, a community of individuals with
a varied picture of strengths and vulnerabilities. Given that we all have
mental health needs to varying degrees at different points in our lives,
when a trauma takes place this is likely to exacerbate our pre-existing
vulnerabilities. In the context of parish life where a priest's task is to
shepherd his flock, his untimely removal, be this through death, a breakdown in relations or other circumstances, is likely to threaten the stability of people's lives, at least in the short term. When a priest's presence,
which a parish has come to expect almost without question, is stripped
away quite suddenly, every member of the parish will be affected, but
particularly those who are already vulnerable.

It is not the purpose of this book to try to presume what the ending
of David's ministry meant to countless individuals. And yet our move to
St Andrew's and the start of Gavin's ministry there did highlight a need,
especially in the early stages, to listen to people's stories. These stories
spoke compellingly not only about the pain and anguish of what had
been, but also of how the people had survived this experience and, in
doing so, had themselves initiated the first stages of the healing process.

This process of healing lent itself in particular to the Liturgy of the
Word which provides unprecedented yet structured space for story-
telling and story-listening through the lectionary readings, the sermon
and the intercessions. Within these structures meaning and purpose can
be found. To have failed to engage in this process would have somehow
exacerbated the pain of what had been, and fixed it in a place which
might unwittingly have denied people their own opportunity of making
sense of the past.

At a secondary level, I too experienced something of the need to
understand and discern the parish's history as we inherited it. When we
first moved into the vicarage, I struggled with my own feelings about the
house's recent past. I realized that my knowledge of what had taken place

was patchy and I was torn between a need to block out and not know and a need to know more. Only as my understanding of David's ministry unfolded – its highs, its lows and its sudden ending – did I start to understand something of what it means to integrate past experience with present living. I realized that the effort of not knowing and not understanding the past, be this for the parish first hand or for myself once removed, was in itself a burden.

This thinking is borne out in the psychoanalytical literature. Garland (1998a) writes: 'Increasingly, clinical findings indicate that events have to be remembered, rather than forgotten or put out of one's mind' (p. 4). She draws upon the experiences of Holocaust survivors as an example:

> In spite of their understandable wish to put the past behind them and to spare their loved ones the knowledge of the worst of what they have been through, it seems in many cases that areas of hidden or denied parental devastation become a burden that may have to be carried unconsciously by the children, even the grandchildren of survivors. (Garland, 1998a, p. 4)

The 'unconscious' nature of this burden is impossible to quantify, and will mean something different to each individual. David did not leave behind children or grandchildren, but he did leave behind a flock who loved and cared for him and who, God willing, will go on to foster countless generations of people who share their lives with St Andrew's church and parish. When Gavin and I moved to St Andrew's, we were, in a sense, the next generation. Though our time there was brief, we hope and pray that our time there was a good one – certainly we shall carry it with us all our days. We hope, in essence, that our time helped remove something of the unconscious burden that I feel we inherited; creating space for new beginnings which at the same time recognized the value of the past.

Understanding expectations and feelings

A new incumbent inevitably arrives with some degree of expectations – expectations placed on him, not only by the new parish but equally so by himself. Moving from a very articulate and middle-class parish, we assumed that these expectations would be all the keener given the context of David's death. Yet one of the particular gifts (and perhaps challenges) of the people of St Andrew's was their very lack of expectation. They welcomed Gavin and me in a way that we will probably never know again. They included us in their lives with an openness and frankness which to this day we miss and long for. Beyond this, however, at one level at least, there were no expectations, at least no expectations for change. Little to no pressure was placed on Gavin to start new services, new initiatives, new anything. The people were happy for him to be present, to be open, and to remain. The expectations were, therefore, primarily self-induced. Inevitably Gavin had his own ideas, beliefs and hopes for the church. Some of these he installed quickly (such as the new liturgy) and those were received well, albeit with a certain passivity. But other initiatives, such as Bible study groups, were often poorly attended. As these initiatives by and large failed to take off, I watched with concern and tried to understand Gavin's despondency.

In one sense, I could relate to what Gavin was feeling. In my own work, how have I felt when, in addition to setting aside time for a session, I have spent time preparing for that session and the client fails to turn up? Frustrated perhaps? Despondent or angry? Relieved? Indifferent? Pragmatic? ('At least now I can catch up on some administration!') And what do I do with these feelings when I experience them? Particularly when, perhaps, I have already met the client once, twice, maybe several times and then they fail to show? What does this say about my skills or the relationship I have established with them? Have I failed them? Have they failed me? How easy or difficult is it to admit to our feelings of being 'let down' when we have put a lot of effort into something?

Within my professional world, my training encourages me to make sense of people's lateness or non-attendance; to try to understand which factors (emotional and/or practical) might be impinging on someone's ability to attend or engage with sessions. Though I am not an automaton and I do have feelings, the boundaries are by and large clear. In many ways, I am buffeted by the NHS – by my professional colleagues, by supervision, by the routine structures that are in place, by the simple fact that, at the end of the day, I close the door behind me and go home. For the parish priest, it seems to me, there is no such cut-off. He does not close the door behind him because the threshold and boundaries of his working life are also the threshold and boundaries of his home life. Erratic attendance at services, late arrivals, the fear of a 'failing' church –

what is a priest to do with his own feelings of disappointment, guilt or even despair? Be we lay or ordained, we need to acknowledge and grapple with these difficult feelings if we are to develop an honest and open understanding of the parish life that we inhabit.

Understanding mental health

One of the very real and lasting challenges for Gavin's ministry at St Andrew's was his struggle to share his passion for the gospel beyond the Sunday Eucharist. As I write this, I can almost hear in my head the paradox of what I am saying. What is more profound, more lasting, more important than the Eucharist itself? Is that not what this book is about when all is said and done: the power of the Eucharist – the potential for it to receive all, contain all and accept all? I seem, therefore, to highlight only my own frailty, my own limited, very human expectations in the dilemma I speak of.

And yet, despite the uncomfortable nature of this paradox, I do believe it is important to try to understand something of the people that a parish priest's community comprises. I remember discussing this with a friend, also a priest in an urban parish. He too was experiencing many of the difficulties that Gavin himself was encountering. I recall his words as he reflected on his own struggles and battles with parish ministry: 'At first I thought people just had issues – I then realized that they weren't just issues, they were real mental health problems.' The breadth of this comment is critical. It is all too easy not to recognize mental health problems when they present themselves, either in ourselves or others. Having identified mental health as an issue, however, the challenge remains how to make sense of it.

*   *   *

I wish to draw again from the psychological model, cognitive behaviour therapy (CBT), and consider how this might inform our understanding of mental health in a parish context. Simply put, CBT is based on the assumption that there is a relationship between what we *think* (cognition), what we *feel* (emotion) and what we *do* about something (action) (Teasdale, 1997, p. 67). For somebody suffering from depression, this might be illustrated as follows: 'I'm useless, nobody likes me' (negative thought); 'I feel miserable and lonely' (negative emotion); 'I can't face leaving the house today' (negative action). A key aspect of CBT is, therefore, to identify negative patterns of thinking, to look at their validity, challenge them and, hopefully, to reverse them. This in turn seeks to change unhelpful patterns of behaviour. Furthermore, as the relationship between cognition and behaviour is seen to be reciprocal, a change in behaviour (for example a person with depression carrying out small household tasks) might also bring about a change in thinking.

The assumptions of CBT seem to have critical value when considering how the model might relate to some challenges of parish life. In relation to Gavin's difficulty in achieving any sizeable or consistent attendance at the various groups he initiated, clearly I cannot account for any internal negative thoughts or beliefs which individuals might have experienced. Yet I cannot help but speculate that, for some at least, individual thought patterns went some way to inhibiting confidence and energy for new initiatives. One hypothesis, therefore, is that underlying negative thoughts included: 'I'm not up to that; I won't know what to say; it's probably not for people like me anyhow', and that this style of thinking led to poor attendance, withdrawal and even apathy among parishioners.

Attending a church activity might sound simple enough. But the matter is not simple if you are anxious, predisposed to thinking you will 'get it wrong' and, if you get it wrong, everything will come crashing down around you. To understand something of this anxiety – of what it means to someone's internal world to suffer from worried, debilitating thoughts – is essential for a parish priest if he is to help enable his community to take responsibility for its own well-being.

Understanding the process of healing

Psychological formulation is a circular process. This process, which enables us constantly to interpret and reinterpret stories as they unfold, is critical to my own understanding of the St Andrew's story, both as we lived in it and retrospectively.

The vicarage was, for me, whether consciously or subconsciously, always an important barometer for my own feelings about St Andrew's. When it came to decorating in the early stages, this process inevitably involved some level of hypothesis testing. What colour would work for which room? Should we stick to a good old mass brand or could we splash out and go for an upgrade? Sample pots went some way to helping these formulations ('Let's try green') and reformulations ('After all, let's not'). The one room, however, that Gavin and I struggled to 'get right' was the lounge/dining room. I forget now at which point I learned that this was the place of David's death. Certainly I did not know it when we first looked round; whether I knew it by the time we moved in, I cannot be sure. Either way, this was the one room the colour of which we could not settle on.

We had started to paint the lounge the day of that first party. We had, between us, chosen two shades of green, and had started to roll on the first coat. Minutes into the task, however, we realized our mistake. The light green, in particular, which was to cover the majority of the walls, was lurid to say the least. We did not need to debate our decision for long. We abandoned the task mid-flight and agreed to return what pots remained, exchanging them for a more subtle shade. This we did and, second time round, we were less vocal in our misgivings. Misgivings we each still had, but neither of us voiced them at this stage. Instead we soldiered through to the bitter end, and only a year into our time there did we reluctantly admit that the colour really didn't work, we would have to start again. Our third attempt was the least ambitious and, in relative terms, the most successful. But again it was only in our last months there that one night, gas-fire lit, trying to get warm, we had a conversation about how difficult it had been to make this room home. I did not like to believe that our uncertainty was in any way linked to the house's history, and yet this was my instinct: a real enough instinct, but one that seemed to contradict my also genuine feeling that the house 'did not have a bad feel'.

I have come to understand the contradictory nature of these feelings more clearly now that we have left St Andrew's. In the early stages of writing this book, a chance telephone conversation took me to the writings of Esther de Waal. Having no primary source to hand, Gavin resorted to the internet on my behalf to learn more about this Christian writer, with specialist fields of the Benedictine Rule and Celtic spirituality. Following a visit to Melbourne to discuss her book, *Lost in Wonder: Rediscovering the Spiritual Art of Attentiveness* (2003), an article written for the Melbourne press described how de Waal 'experiences life intensely as a gift'. This gift, it goes on to say, is realized in her belief in the importance of praise and wonder for all things.

As somebody who falls short of giving praise on a daily basis, I read the article with more discomfort than wonder. It spoke powerfully to me throughout, but it was the article's closing two paragraphs that made a particular impression on me. These revealed that, while de Waal celebrates life as a gift, she also suffers from depression. The article finishes by quoting de Waal herself:

> As someone who suffers from recurrent depression I am so tired of having Mother Julian quoted at me – 'all will be well and all manner of things will be well', because when you are actually at the bottom of a very dark tunnel and there is no daylight at all at the end, that is the last thing you want to hear.
>
> Ultimately there can only be one point of reference and that is making the whole paschal mystery a reality for oneself, and continuing to believe that against all the odds new life can flow out of darkness and pain. However, pain and darkness don't disappear and I am so glad that the resurrected Christ had wounded hands and wounded feet.

These lines at one level recapitulate the basic tenet of the Christian faith: the Easter story is one that triumphs on paradox; through the most terrible suffering, new life is born. 'We have to believe in the resurrection', Gavin said to me when we first discussed moving into the vicarage, a statement delivered then over a drink in a Fulham pub. I had heard the words and I had listened to them, but they did not really register. Why, then, did these lines of de Waal's register so acutely? Timing and place, I suppose, were important. They somehow gave me permission at a distance to articulate what I had felt but had not understood during my three years at St Andrew's: 'pain and darkness do not disappear . . .' After all, 'the resurrected Christ had wounded hands and feet'.

This image spoke profoundly about the house as we inherited it. The house became central to my understanding of our time at St Andrew's because my relationship to it seemed to reflect something of the healing process itself. Yes, it was a good house, it was a great house. It was a house of many rooms and many stages. We would grow to love it and call it our home. When the parish came to visit, it would be filled above all with great life and vitality. We would feel again that we were Easter people; that the resurrection was among us. But we would not forget. Of course we should not forget. The lounge in its redecorated form – the different shades of green, the windows scrubbed and the curtains hung – was daily testimony to this unending paradox of renewed life and unfaded suffering. The paradoxical image, therefore, of the risen Christ does not so much speak as cry out for the story of mental health and healing.

Integrating Mind and Spirit (Part 4)

Listening and meaning

A theistic approach to life quite deliberately perceives, analyses and inter-prets the world as the manifestation of the divine. All relationships, all encounters, all histories are determined for the theist, and in our case Chris-tians, by a sense of sacred narrative – the story of God's people. Psychology's place in this narrative is necessarily tentative; it can, though, offer an insight into the biological, psychological and social factors which inform Christian journeys, past and present. Our experience of mental health is one perspective that underpins these journeys. How we understand the rela-tionship between our thoughts, feelings and behaviour; how we interpret the burdens and traumas of our past to impact on our present; these are just two ways in which we might seek to deepen our psychological understand-ing of our Christian journey.

On the one hand, pastoral ministry seeks to communicate the existence of a loving God, the author of all life. On the other, it recognizes the anguish of mental health problems, shattering the panacea that faith brings peace and tranquility in all things. The story of God in human form presents a different story: that God is present in the disturbance of mental health and the suffering it manifests.

Practical implications

A priest's challenge is somehow to recognize when an individual has mental health difficulties. To reiterate, a priest is not being asked to rein-vent himself and start thinking or behaving like a psychologist or any other mental health practitioner in these scenarios. Hopefully, though, a few brief insights will equip him with some ways of listening more attentively when hearing people's stories of mental health disturbance.

Awareness

Clearly it is not a priest's role to try to diagnose the nature of an individual's mental health problems. It is helpful, though, to be aware of the range of mental health difficulties. These include: mood problems (depression and bi-polar disorder); anxiety problems (e.g. generalized anxiety disorder, panic disorder, obsessive compulsive disorder, post-traumatic stress disorder and social phobia); physical health problems (e.g. somatoform disorder, chronic pain, adjustment to illness, eating disorders and substance abuse) and other psychological difficulties (e.g. schizophrenia, borderline personality disorder and anger management difficulties) (summary adapted from Carr and McNulty, 2006).

How the encounter makes you feel

Mental health problems in others can impact greatly on how we feel in a given situation, both consciously and unconsciously. Feelings might include: fear, ambivalence, uncertainty, frustration, feelings of helplessness or uselessness, of being overwhelmed. In recognizing how we feel when asked to respond to mental health difficulties in others, this can give us an insight into how the individual is feeling as well as those key people around that individual (for example family members or friends, other professionals). These feelings can also highlight our own frailties and vulnerabilities.

Understanding the triggers or antecedents to an individual's difficulties

When trying to make sense of another's story, it can be helpful to try to understand the pattern of behaviours relating to an individual's mental health difficulties. In very simple terms, finding out, for example, that recent marital difficulties have led to a breakdown in mental health can help inform decisions about how best to intervene – referral to Relate, for example.

Note: Mindfulness about safety to oneself or others may be pertinent. In these instances, therapeutic ideas about healing are not appropriate and a more immediate course of action needs to be taken. Reference to diocesan guidelines for good practice is essential.

Understanding of negative thought patterns

According to cognitive behaviour therapy, an individual experiencing depression will be experiencing two kinds of negative thoughts: 'negative automatic thoughts' and 'underlying dysfunctional assumptions'. 'Negative automatic thoughts' are triggered by any perceived threat or difficult scenario, for example 'I can't do this' or 'I knew I wouldn't know anybody here.' These negative automatic thoughts are based on our 'underlying dysfunctional assumptions', possibly rooted in childhood, for example 'I'm worthless, I'm useless, nobody likes me.'

Understanding of consequences

An individual with mental health problems is not an island but part of a system of people and relationships. How we respond to their difficulties in turn affects them. For example, if they are anxious and we allow them to become overly dependent on our support, we are not in the long run helping them but in fact feeding their anxiety. Conversely, if we ignore their cry for help, we may simply reinforce their sense of isolation and so exacerbate their vulnerability.

Understanding of risk to oneself

When trying to make sense of an individual's presenting difficulties, it may be necessary to be selective with the information and make some key decisions. A question that can be helpful in guiding this process is: Given what I am witnessing and hearing, given the history of this situation/person or its unfamiliarity, do I as an individual feel safe? Clergy safety is a whole topic in itself and cannot be covered here. Two essential resources are: 'Knocking at Heaven's Door: Challenges and Opportunities Presented by the Casual Caller in the Parish' (CARIS, 1996), and National Churchwatch ('Personal Safety Advice Factsheet'), both available on the internet (see Bibliography).

National Churchwatch flags up ten 'top tips' to help protect clergy safety – see reference and website for details. Pointers are summarized as follows: trust your instincts; know your limitations; always report incidents; keep calm; plan ahead; report any area of your work that puts you at risk; know what the rules are, not what you think they are; never be afraid to run away; no item of property or building is worth your life; be afraid, not paranoid.

Understanding of risk to others

Based on what the individual is telling me, their body language and level of agitation, do I think the individual is at risk of harming either himself or herself or others? If the answer to either of these questions is 'Yes' (however tentative), again ideas about therapeutic healing are suspended and measures need to be implemented to protect individual(s) concerned. For example, inform key agencies such as police, social services and health (for example GP, psychiatry); and follow up these contacts wherever possible.

Consider forums in which these issues might helpfully be discussed and explored. For example, local collaboration with neighbouring clergy to offer peer supervision and support.

Questions for individual reflection and/or discussion

1. Which parts of the Christian story speak to you about mental health?
2. What does the Gerasene demoniac represent to you? If you were to encounter him today, how might you respond to him?
3. In what ways might our interpretation of biblical stories help us better understand our relationships with one another?
4. How does an understanding of mental health inform your church community? How might this understanding deepen your awareness of the presence of God?

A prayer of the Word

Incarnate Word
you share your life with all humanity.
You are God's eternal presence in his creation.
As we respond to the scriptures past,
so too we cry for your saving help today.
In our poverty, feed us with your wisdom;
teach us, affirm us, pray for us,
now and evermore.
Amen.

Part 5

Transformations

The following two chapters explore the challenges of parish life in the context of mental health and healing. Chapter 9, at one level, tells the story of frustrated initiatives and failure in a new parochial ministry. This story is set against the backdrop of Rublev's icon of the Holy Trinity which can be seen to be a window into the transformative nature of the Eucharist.

Chapter 10 focuses on a series of case studies in both the clinical and parish setting. The studies are seen from a psychological perspective and parallels are drawn between the gradual process of healing and therapeutic change in both contexts. In this way various themes are explored, including personal and parish renewal, and liaison with other caring professionals.

Chapter 9

The Liturgy of the Sacrament

The sacrament of welcome

'The Eucharist is a healing service par excellence' (Archbishops' Council, 2000, p. 269). The liturgy of the Eucharist describes the nature of God's Trinity, taking the community of believers on a pilgrimage which offers sanctity, wholeness and ultimately liberation. The priest at the altar is graced with the responsibility of creating holy space in which the presence of God through the priesthood of believers is to be welcomed. The sacredness of the occasion results from the discipline and devotion of years of prayer and worship across generations of faith in the Judeo-Christian tradition.

At St Andrew's Church, Fulham Fields, this particular holy space was marked by the icon of the Holy Trinity which hovered above the nave altar. Andrei Rublev's fifteenth-century window into the nature of God was one of the most significant internal features of the church. Hung by translucent wire from the rafters of the nave, the three angels in the icon appeared to be loitering with the intention of welcoming the stranger in the pew to the holy table. The icon takes as its inspiration the story of the visitation of three strangers to Abraham and Sarah. Abraham, the father of monotheistic faith, instinctively treated these visitors as divine beings of the one God; his welcome was heartfelt and sincere. He brought his guests water to clean themselves and food that they might be refreshed – not just any food but freshly baked cakes and a choice calf. Rublev conveys the meal in a eucharistic setting with a cup (chalice) and the sacrificed animal positioned on the table for all to share. Abraham and Sarah celebrate the feast, not knowing that their lives are to be totally transformed. Their vulnerability – the theme of barrenness – was to be re-framed by God. The opportunity to change, which is God's grace in our daily lives, is a gift which not only heralds new faith for Abraham and Sarah, it also heralds new faith in us. This *metanoia*, changing the way in which we perceive ourselves and life, is at the heart of the eucharistic celebration.

From the priest's perspective, looking from the altar to the congregation in the nave, it was possible to see another aspect of Rublev's iconography. The drama of the visitation – the roles of Abraham, Sarah and that of the strangers – could be seen to be played out Sunday by Sunday at St Andrew's by those who occupied the holy space of the nave. Those who felt strong and in command of themselves played the angels' role – delivering hope and comfort. Those who felt weak and in need of emotional health and mental fitness reflected the pain of the childless Abraham and Sarah – desiring direction, nurture and support. The reality of mental health was made present by a substantial number who attended the church. The altar was therefore surrounded by a divine presence, of the God who shares strength and weakness, hope and loss, togetherness and brokenness. In the holy space created by the eucharistic feast, God calls his people together to care for one another. This meeting place, this holy space was an authentic expression of God's Holy Trinity. God provides a space for all to share in this sacramental environment. God makes himself present to us, God calls us to the feast, friends and strangers alike.

Abraham's visitors did not just create holiness, they also provided holiness. The strangers were able to contain the suffering of Abraham and Sarah, they listened to their story. The encounter between these strangers, between God and his people, recognized the presence of both pain and potential. The wonder of the story is that, through this engagement between divinity and humanity, a transformation occurred in the lives of Abraham and Sarah. Again this is the sacramental nature of the rite of the Eucharist: it reconciles difference and transforms it into hope.

The Gospel writer Luke adopts this hope-filled theology throughout his writings about the life and teachings of Jesus, but nowhere more transparently than in the Parable of the Great Feast. In this story Jesus alludes to the heavenly banquet which will be shared with the whole of God's people. Jesus describes the 'upside down-ness' of God's kingdom, the shocking reality that God calls the weak, the lame, the distressed, the ostracized of society. God sets the rules and the etiquette for his kingdom which shakes us out of our human conviction that success is driven by achievement. Jesus' teaching and Luke's theology, which validates the divine status of each and every human being, characterized the essential nature of the St Andrew's experience. It is no surprise to learn that St Andrew's was at its very best when the people shared in feasting. The Agape after the Eucharist, held on selected occasions, was something to behold. Exotic food and ample drink were supplied by the people for the people.

The Parable of the Great Feast demonstrates the gospel imperative of sacrificial love, of including others even when that inclusion becomes the harder task. St Andrew's Church was – and still is! – known locally as a welcoming, inclusive community. Welcoming people into the sacred space of the church was simply to accept them without condition, to befriend them and kindle the spark of faith within them. One of the church's strengths was to welcome the underdog, the scarred and the lonely, to regard those strangers as friends. Many found faith at St Andrew's as a result, the Eucharist being the defining rite of the church that shaped their belief and practice.

The sacrament of failure

Despite the obvious importance of the weekly eucharistic gathering, I quickly became aware of the 'Sunday-only' culture at St Andrew's. I thought this to be a weakness. The Sunday Eucharist, as in many parish churches, was the benchmark for health at St Andrew's. Parish ministry should flow from this one event. Sunday morning was the time when the people of the parish of Fulham Fields came to the table, when a welcome was provided, when cleansing could be administered, when refreshment was given and good news received. The community at St Andrew's came alive on Sunday. In addition to the Eucharist, all PCC meetings, standing committees and fellowship (including Sunday 'breakfast' or lunch) took place on the sabbath day. The work of the church was, therefore, very much bound up by this one hectic Sunday gathering. The continuum of prayer, work and fellowship, living the Christ-life seven days a week, not one out of seven, was not practised, although I maintained the daily office with a faithful few both morning and evening.

New initiatives were launched in an effort to bring to life the gospel at different times and in different places. I was keen to bring people together in various ways – be this to share in fellowship during the week or explore their faith outside the structures of the Eucharist. I hoped the new initiatives offered some realistic starting points for parish renewal. However, these were not always received with enthusiasm, and to begin with I could not understand why.

I first set up the 'Sandwich Club'. I wanted to appeal to the lonely by offering lunch at the vicarage once a week. I thought this might be a way of bringing strangers together in an informal environment. It would also help to provide a table where stories could be shared and encounters made. I publicized the Sandwich Club in the Sunday newsletter, making it clear that I would be providing the sandwiches. After a hopeful start, however, this new initiative quickly fell by the wayside.

Another attempt to make holy space was what I called the 'Spirituality Clinic'. I promised that every Wednesday morning I would be available to any folk who had questions about their faith or life in general. Like a doctor in general practice, I was a professional carer in a busy city corner in the midst of the working week, waiting to be visited by anyone who had need to use this service. The Spirituality Clinic failed, its waiting room, the vicarage lounge, was left unattended.

At times I associated this non-attendance with general apathy, at other times with a deeper underlying fragility that the community expressed. St Andrew's, like any other church across the land, comprised a great variety of people, some of whom displayed signs of emotional need, others who coped more readily with all that life had to offer. One consequence, however, of this emotional need seemed to manifest itself in the difficulty of encouraging a greater sense of discipleship and witness to the gospel. Engaging the parish in new initiatives was not the only stumbling block I encountered. There were no lay readers, no house groups, no prayer groups. The rota for Sunday duties was in danger of imploding through lack of interest. It seemed that it fell to a few to take on board responsibility and ownership for their church.

I was keen for the parish of Fulham Fields to explore the reasons for this apathy, and to try to get to the root cause of it. I was very aware that other priests in the deanery seemed to be energized by various projects that they had undertaken, and saw what lay and clerical support seemed to offer them. Wanting the same for St Andrew's, I decided to set up an 'Away Day' in a venue outside the parish as a means of exploring how we might go about this. In simple terms, I called the church for a health check. The 'Growing Healthy Churches' material (Warren and Hodgson, 2001) had become a popular resource in the diocese. It was an integral element of the mission-action planning of the churches of the area. I was keen to explore the possibilities of the Healthy Church criteria and relate them to St Andrew's, Fulham Fields.[1] The desire to form a healthy church was also articulated by the Desert Fathers and Mothers of the fourth and fifth centuries. As Rowan Williams writes:

> A healthy church is one in which we seek to stay connected with God by seeking to connect others with God . . . A church that is living in such a way is the only church that will have anything *different* to say to the world. (2003, p. 34)

Most of the Away Day's outcomes consisted of aspirational targets, a wish-list that in itself spoke about where the St Andrew's community was at. A steering group was appointed to implement the following recommendations:

1.   Develop small group networks for prayer/Bible study, courses and events.
2.   Pray towards the creation of a healing ministry.
3.   Develop closer community links, in particular with local council estates.
4.   Create a meditation/prayer group to pray for God's blessing on all future plans.
5.   Develop the laity to lead and minister.

As I look back at these recommendations now, I recall the difficulties of translating these ideas into practice. Nonetheless, the day was a huge success. It was hoped that the occasion might set a precedent for the future. It got people out of the parish to have fellowship together and to think strategically about the future of 'their church'. What was more, all the recommendations had been made holding the Eucharist at the heart of all that we were trying to achieve.

One of the clear outcomes to the Healthy Church process was that, if St Andrew's was to model itself upon the eucharistic rite, it needed to become a risk-taking church. The diocese was quite rightly insisting upon greater accountability among its priests, especially in terms of paying into the Common Fund (the share of money needed to finance and house the clergy in a parish as well as to nurture and facilitate the wider diocese). St Andrew's aspired to pay its way but was unable to, despite increases to its electoral roll and numbers of communicants. The wealth of resources that many of my neighbouring colleagues had at their disposal, both human and monetary, was striking in comparison to St Andrew's. For example, St Andrew's was left open to the public by day and had been pilfered of all of its treasures. When the ancient boiler blew, an almighty fundraising effort went into financing a replacement. But it was actually the lack of human resource that was so crippling to mission growth. I decided to approach one of my wealthiest, evangelical neighbours in a spirit of ecumenical zeal. I mapped out my vision of a parish church which was rooted in sacramental worship and inspired by charismatic gifts. I contacted the church in question and audaciously proposed a marriage. The early courtship was promising but the engagement was soon to end. My neighbour wanted autonomy, I wanted a union. The St Andrew's PCC was ready and able to take a risk and showed great humility in allowing such a venture to be discussed. There was a simple desire to seek and serve God in reverence and dignity. Unfortunately, nothing was born out of the affair.

The area bishop through his oversight was clear about my remit for the parish of Fulham Fields. He wanted the church congregation better to reflect the demography of the parish. Personal networking, pastoral services and publicity made some impact but, in competitive terms, St Andrew's was a failing church. I hoped that my evangelical neighbour would help in this mission. On reflection I feared it saw St Andrew's as a poisoned chalice. This was the place which had a traumatic past, and many wondered about its future. The catholic–charismatic venture was a kingdom opportunity, to listen to one another, to share in the Eucharist and, in doing so, in God's sacrificial giving of his own life. Many in the world see this sacrifice as failure. Indeed 'failure' is a loaded word even in ecclesiastical circles. I was to learn a great deal from the complexities of developing partnerships with churches of different theological integrities.

With the benefit of hindsight and some distance, I now feel more able to consider the possible reasons for the 'failure' of these varied attempts at growth. The health of the parish at the time simply could not sustain such new initiatives. My own ambition of creating a 'successful' church was obstructing the real source of need – the need for the people to be given time and space in which to be loved. St Andrew's, Fulham Fields, was in need of a base to build from. This base was, I now understand, the Sunday Eucharist itself.

The sacrament of healing

Given that healing permeates the liturgy of the Eucharist, the rite can be described as a sacrament of transformation, giving opportunity for change to occur. The church of St Andrew's was, at this particular stage of its journey, developing a sense of therapeutic awareness, placing a greater emphasis upon prayer and creating an atmosphere of positive containment. At St Andrew's the Eucharist offered healing to both mind and spirit. I was to discover how its healing depth transformed the sacred spaces of the lives of God's people. Despite my need for children's workers and missioners, despite the crumbling spire and the broken windows, the Eucharist told its own story week by week of *metanoia*, the transformation of the ordinary into something divine. Hope was being graced by God and not as a result of my own attempts to achieve 'success'.

The icon of the Trinity and its symbolic events was a constant reminder of such hope. Its implication for my own ministry seemed clear: to gather the people together. Only by gathering together could we fully welcome and witness God's presence in our lives. Sunday therefore became an even greater feast, an occasion when we could celebrate our differences and bring to God our brokenness too. It was as though my planning and manipulation of initiatives and events had been masking the process of healing. My lesson was to see the expansiveness of God's presence, to see the 'God of small things',[2] to marvel at the minutiae, even the humdrum of parish life.

In order to develop St Andrew's further as a community, I had to make Sunday a day of renewal. It was important not to bombast the parish with new initiatives which it was not ready to grasp. In short, I needed to ensure that the Sunday gathering was a place of feeding and healing. It was therefore essential that the Eucharist remained the one occasion in a busy week that would be unchanged, consistently offering fellowship, guidance and freedom. Sunday morning was purposefully targeted as the time for growth and renewal.

Growth did indeed result. This was witnessed through the proliferation of baptisms, the reformation of the 'Children's Church', the numbers of communicants, as well as those offering to read, serve, intercess and sing. New members of the PCC were found, and this gave the church fresh direction. Sunday mornings became the hub of all parish activity, especially the fellowship that took place after the Eucharist. Given time, more resources could well have been invested into other initiatives throughout the week. But the church was not ready for these. The Sunday Eucharist was the focus of fellowship and care. Sunday had to be carefully planned and delivered. I had invested a great deal in developing the liturgy. If this was to be the first stage of parish renewal, it had to be right; it had to fulfil the criteria of a healthy church.

The sacrament of transformation

The Eucharist lies at the heart of any sacred space because within it God becomes present to his people. From simple matter (bread and wine) through the agency of the Holy Spirit, God is made real before the people of God. Just as the angels/strangers brought word of life to Abraham and Sarah, so too the invocation of the Holy Spirit brings forth life from ordinary matter. Frances Young echoes this thought:

> The Eucharist, as centred in the Great Thanksgiving Prayer, is not just about atonement or spiritual feeding, or Real Presence. It is about the whole overarching narrative which gives us a sense of our place in things, beginning with creation. (2001, p. 86)

St Andrew's Church was witness to God's sacredness. The sacred space was in part co-created by the people – the welcomers, the sacristan, the musicians, the choir, the readers, the intercessors, the acolytes, the crucifer. All these played their part in creating the space for all to enter. This is the empty space within Rublev's icon, its emptiness demands life to fill it. The empty space begs our hospitality and welcome. The icon ushers a call to community: God's greatest desire that we love one another as he loves us.

What we actually witnessed at St Andrew's during these eucharistic encounters was the fullness of Christ, alive to those who shared their story with God. It was difficult not to get caught up in a celebratory joy. Perhaps we were celebrating a kind of change, of transformation, each time that we came together. It was as though all things were absorbed –

all ills, needs and fears. The community at St Andrew's was literally living out a tension, forming the bond between our humanity and God's loving. Immersed in this divine love, God's children are accepted with unconditional regard. Suspended in time, we are given a moment of blessedness as God's visitation on his people brings the divine alongside our failings and becomes the generous host of the feast. We are made more real through this state of grace, through this 'being in relationship'.

At the time of the fraction in the Eucharist – the breaking of Christ's body for his people to share – we give thanks that our humanity, our disability and our dysfunction may also be shared by God. This is what God intended, for his creation to share in all of life's resources, gifts and burdens: 'though we are many, we are one body, because we all share in one bread'.[3] At the altar table, we bring together our separateness and seek out hope. This is the place where Christ transcends despair and proclaims 'See, I am making all things new' (Revelation 21.5). As the people of St Andrew's entered the circle of believers to receive the sacrament, all were accorded an unconditional welcome. Many of those who responded to the invitation to feast at the table were battered and worn by much that life and circumstance had thrown at them. Yet we were all deeply connected; we had a common cause, a shared vision.

The icon continued to gaze upon the people of St Andrew's. Rublev's Holy Trinity related to all that we shared, all of our failures and successes, our hurts and feelings. The power of the Eucharist, we discovered, could not be restricted by people, institutions, time or space. This was the very essence of the pilgrimage to God. It offered welcome to the lost, health to the sick, humility to the strong and transformation to all who call upon the name of God. The Eucharist gave to those disturbed by mind and spirit a source of life which God has ordained to be the gift of the Christian Church. This perfect gift of love is simply God's offering of himself which deserves our thanks. So what we did experience in those three short years was a eucharistic experience: taking the broken people and sharing their lives in all of their complexities and giving thanks to God for our communion together.

Chapter 10

Psychological Intervention

A new ministry and new interventions

The term 'intervention' is somewhat crude and not one that I sit altogether comfortably with. Nonetheless it is one that, in my professional life, I have grown up with, and it does seem to have relevance here. In psychological terms, intervention refers to the way in which we work with or 'treat' a client. At the heart of its process lies the potential for, and journey towards, therapeutic change.

What bearing might this process of psychological intervention have on parish life? Care, healing, renewal, transformation: these are all key tenets of the sacrament of the Eucharist – key objectives of any parochial ministry. At times they might be hard to see; at other times we might not believe we are anywhere near them; but they are there, visible and invisible, working their way out in the everyday of parish life. As a clinical psychologist, I have frequently struggled with what it is that I am 'doing'. Am I doing the right thing? Am I helping? Does my client think I am helping? Am I being 'psychological' or is it just plain common sense? The questions seem to demand concrete answers. But sometimes it is as well to sit lightly with these questions. As already established, there can be no certainties when it comes to the business of 'healing', psychological or spiritual.

I had my first lesson in underestimating what it is to 'be psychological' several years ago when I started out as a trainee. After some careful discussion and supervision, my supervisor sent me off on a series of home visits to work with a lady, Dee, in her fifties who had suffered a stroke. While she remained physically able, this had affected some aspects of her short-term memory which in turn impacted on her ability to organize her domestic and financial arrangements. Having previously managed a large department, her stroke had had considerable impact on her self-esteem and general mood. She started to feel worthless, unable to cope, and lost confidence in the skills she still had.

My brief was to work with Dee over a course of weeks, seeking to engage her in developing ideas and strategies for managing her life in the light of her new disability. In many ways I acted as her prompt and her encourager, reminding her which types of tasks she needed to carry out in order to aid her independence. Over the weeks we established a series of systems to help her with the daily running of her life. Once set up, we inevitably discovered new glitches to its smooth operation and I would suggest simple ways of intervening. My suggestions were far from earth-shattering and at times I felt concerned that I might seem patronizing, but our relationship was based on collaborative thinking and mutual respect and we seemed to make progress.

The benefits of my work with Dee were apparent from quite early on: her mood and self-esteem improved and, despite some ongoing set-backs, she did indeed start to manage her life more successfully. Despite this, I recall with shame that, after the first few weeks, I started to feel frustrated about my role in Dee's recovery. After some hesitancy, I took this frustration to supervision and tried to articulate that I felt I was not really being stretched – anyone could do what I was doing. Could I perhaps have a case which allowed me to work more 'psychologically' next time? I remember that my supervisor smiled. 'Don't you realize, Jo, that what you are doing is very psychological?' I frowned. She quizzed me again about my understanding of Dee's difficulties, how they had come about, in what way her beliefs and negative thought patterns had been impacting on her ability to utilize the resources she had, and what factors I thought might precipitate a relapse. I responded at some length, only partially aware of what I was conceding. When I had finished, though, I remember I laughed. Perhaps it was true after all. Perhaps the way in which I had been thinking, and therefore what I was doing, had been more 'psychological' than I had realized.

*   *   *

Some of my early frustrations as a trainee remind me in retrospect of Gavin's own ministry at St Andrew's. He had inherited a community whose many gifts, not least their warmth and openness, were under-pinned also by a varied spectrum of vulnerability and mental health needs. This quality of brokenness and disturbance, combined with its unique potential for healing and transformation, is perhaps what drew us to St Andrew's, what nurtured us, challenged us and also at times had the potential for breaking us.

Why could we not, I sometimes now ask myself, partake in those shared gifts of brokenness and transformation to a fuller degree? What was it that prevented us from living out the passion story day in, day out, of allowing ourselves simply to love and be loved, to disappoint and be disappointed? It was in part, I think, because of our desire 'to move things on', for Gavin's desire to embark on new initiatives and 'grow a healthy church', for my desire to see Gavin fulfilled and sustained by his daily ministry. With hindsight, I think perhaps we underestimated the task of entering a place where brokenness and disturbance played such a key part: both on account of the trauma the St Andrew's people had experienced through David's death; and also through their own individual vulnerabilities that preceded this event. Despite some understanding of this, we struggled, at least at one level, to find a way forward.

Gavin's early days at St Andrew's were taken up with implementing various practical steps and initiatives to make the daily running and sacramental life of the church a little more 'water-tight'. It is inevitable that any new incumbent will bring to his post new ideas, in part informed by his own beliefs and inspirations which, ideally in collabora-tion with his PCC and congregation, he will then seek to put in motion. Gavin was no exception, and he has already described some of his early initiatives. Other interventions were of a more domestic nature and included: closing the church at night for security reasons; clearing out a large amount of 'clutter' which was no longer in use from the sacristy; asking members of the congregation to sign up to a cleaning rota; raising the money for a new boiler; and approaching the organization New Deal for Communities (NDC) for funds for a new church path and railings.

It was easy at the time to underestimate the importance of this early 'tidying up' process; to relegate its status somehow to one of house-keeping duties which needed to be got through and endured before the 'real work' could begin. Certainly I am the first to appreciate that being called out to look at a boiler or cleaning up a sacristy with the lone, albeit staunch, unfailing support of one's sacristan, might seem a little frustrating in the context of a new incumbent's wider hopes and vision. The process does, however, at least with hindsight, remind me of my own tendency to overlook how practical interventions might relate to the psychological, emotional and spiritual well-being of an individual – or, in this case, an institution. Given this formulation, it seems that many of Gavin's earlier, practical interventions were central to the new phase in the story of St Andrew's in which the community could move forward and be renewed in a way which gave the people a stronger, more contained base from which to grow.

Creating a 'successful church'

To what extent does this process of taking small, practical steps fit with ideas of creating a 'successful church'? In other words, what part do these steps play in the wider vision or targets awaiting a new parish ministry? In my own work, services are constantly being asked to account for their waiting list times, the management of their resources and personnel, the outcome of their interventions, and so on. This need for accountability, necessary but complicated, is not confined to the NHS. A parish priest may not have waiting-list targets or government initiatives to contend with, but, as the Church is under increasing pressure to be financially viable, he is similarly being asked, overtly or covertly, to adhere to a success-driven ethos of management-speak, head-counting and competition with other, possibly more 'successful' churches. It is important to remember that this growing managerial ethos places expectation and pressure not only on the priest but potentially on the people also.

As I look back at our time at St Andrew's now, I consider the tension played out between the need to pastor people, many of whom were vulnerable, many of whom had experienced first hand the loss of their former priest, and the need to justify one's own ministry, to adhere to a greater model of success-driven management-speak. This tension appeared to manifest itself in many aspects of the life of St Andrew's. It was present in the need, on the one hand, to stand still and care for, to allow God's grace simply to do its work; on the other, to move things forward and generate visible signs of the community's growth. These signs, though, are likely to be gradual and fragile, particularly in the context of a community which is in many ways vulnerable and has suffered some kind of bereavement or trauma. When the Church sets itself specific targets and takes into account the social, economic and ethnic demographics of a parish, does it also take into account, place value on, the mental health needs of those parishioners, the recent history of that parish, and how these factors might stand in conflict with a more concrete model of success and growth? If we fail to consider these factors, we are in danger of thinking of a parish community merely as a whole and forgetting the many parts which form its sum.

The unique value of each and every individual is a basic Christian tenet which is borne out in psychoanalytical thinking. 'To take care of the group is to take care of the individuals within the group' (Bion, 1961, paraphrased by Garland, 1998c, p. 188). This connection between an individual's and a group's well-being seems particularly pertinent in a parish setting. A parish priest has a duty of care to individuals as well as the parish as a whole. He is required, therefore, to reflect not only on the psychological needs of individual parishioners, but also on how these needs might be met within the parish system. In practical terms, this is likely to mean collaboration and partnership with other communities in the parish system.

Mental health and the parish system

Promoting Mental Health (2004) places considerable emphasis on the importance of better partnership between different organizations: 'There are a number of potential benefits of increasing partnership working between statutory and voluntary and community services and faith communities to provide support for people with mental health problems' (p. 55). It summarizes these benefits as follows: an increased awareness within services; an increased understanding about mental health issues for those working in faith communities; and the ability to locate appropriate services. The following two pastoral illustrations help illustrate some key issues which stem from collaborative working with other agencies in the context of parish ministry.

Maureen was well known to the community of St Andrew's. Though her attendance at church had become increasingly erratic following David's death and during the interregnum, she had established regular contact with several priests in neighbouring parishes whom she called upon at all hours for emotional and spiritual assistance.

Maureen suffered from a series of obsessions and compulsions. At an immediate level these expressed a need for hygiene and cleanliness in particular areas of her life. Her underlying anxiety, however, seemed to relate to a fear about not being able to cope and, in the worst eventuality, of dying alone. An isolated figure, her anxiety was further characterized by a need for constant reassurance and support from a range of people within the community, both professional and lay. This anxiety clearly had an infectious quality as, in addition to local clergy, many people in the parish were actively involved in Maureen's welfare. As such they responded to her cries for help with an urgency which, in the long term, far from reducing her anxiety, was unwittingly reinforcing her belief that she could not cope alone.

Early on in Gavin's ministry at St Andrew's, he received an answerphone message from Maureen. Still sharing a telephone line at this stage, we played the message back, having returned from a walk. The voice we heard was one of pain and confusion: in one breath Maureen welcomed Gavin and myself into the vicarage; in the next she said she was fearful she would hurt herself in some way if Gavin did not visit her immediately.

As Gavin gave the situation some thought, I struggled with my own feelings. Based on the little I knew of Maureen's history she was not, it seemed, at risk of harming herself, but her emotional needs were plentiful and it seemed important to establish a helpful precedent from the start. After some hesitation, Gavin contacted one of the churchwardens to find out the current situation. A brief telephone call established that Maureen had in fact already had two visitors that day and that, to all intents and purposes, she was faring well. Following this information, Gavin decided to telephone Maureen in person and arrange to visit her, not immediately as she had requested, but the next day.

When Gavin did meet with Maureen, it was the start of a positive and ongoing relationship. This was partly informed by some boundaries that Gavin placed around the level and frequency of their contact from the outset. Through once-weekly scheduled visits and telephone calls – in time with greater intervals in between – he sought to establish a more contained model of pastoral care. This included encouraging Maureen to attend services which were 'quieter' and therefore less threatening to her (for example, the weekday Eucharist). In this way Maureen's confidence in settings outside her control was increased in small, graded steps. It also had the effect of reducing her isolation and need to make demands on others.

Though Maureen's telephone calls would continue to punctuate our daily and sometimes nocturnal lives at St Andrew's, in time she ceased her demands for immediate assistance and even developed a wry humour in relation to Gavin's scheduled visits and calls. With Maureen's permission, Gavin also sought to collaborate with other agencies, including her GP and psychiatrist. This enabled a network of people to develop a shared understanding of her difficulties and how best to support her. It went some way towards containing Maureen's anxiety, as well as the responses of those around her.

The importance of liaison with other services in the context of mental health is increasingly being recognized by the Church, and should indeed inform parish strategic thinking (see *Promoting Mental Health*, 2004). Contact with other services must only be made after obtaining permission from the individual or responsible adult in question. The important exception to this rule is of course when concerns about an individual's safety, either to him/herself or others, need to take precedence over confidentiality. However, the potential nuances and complexities involved are not always considered. It is not enough simply to know who to liaise with or refer to. Liaison and referral can have sensitive implications.

A parish priest occupies a unique position in the professional–lay network surrounding an individual parishioner with mental health needs. The benefits of a priest entering a professional system have already been considered. What, though, of the pitfalls in this scenario? How might an individual feel when his or her parish priest suggests linking with a system of professionals about which he or she feels potentially ambivalent, even threatened? What does this do to the confidence and trust hopefully established, and how might this sensitivity be handled? Open and straightforward communication, if at all possible, is essential here between priest and parishioner.

The complexities of inter-agency working in parish ministry remind me of an unusual situation several years ago when Gavin was curate and I was on placement locally as a trainee. I had been asked by one of the child psychotherapists, Karen, to attend the case conference of a teenage girl whose parents were known to me through church. Understanding that it would not be appropriate for me to attend, I explained the reasons behind this to my psychotherapy colleague. After some consideration, Karen thought it might be appropriate to invite Gavin to the conference, if the family were happy for this. The suggestion seemed commonsense enough and even reinforced my own assumption that a place 'in the system' is better than no place at all. Karen quickly challenged this assumption, however, by raising the following questions: How might Gavin's presence at the case conference impact on his relationship with the different family members in the everyday doings of parish life? Would they still feel able to turn to him on an informal basis if he was seen to 'align' himself with the professional network? And what might this do to the family's sense of security with him? After careful discussion with the family, Gavin did attend the case conference, but the issues raised by the question of his attendance were a keen lesson for me.

Trauma and the power of the Eucharist

It is only as I write that I start to comprehend something of the enormity of a parish priest's task. If, as is declared at his or her licensing, it is 'to care for the people of this parish in the name of Christ' (Kuhrt, 1997, p. 3), then what, I find myself asking, is the primary task of the church community that he is licensed to minister to? I turn to Gavin for assistance and find he is ready with a response: 'To make disciples of Christ', he replies briefly. For my part, I am disappointed with what he has given me. 'No, I meant something simpler than that really' I retort, and resume my own thoughts.

I realize I am struggling with the far-reaching, somewhat abstract nature of a church's task as Gavin has defined it. In my own work, I would perhaps more naturally quantify what I do: direct and indirect work with clients, report writing and other administration, teaching and supervision – all these somehow embody the primary task of what we do to function as a mental health service. Underpinning this is, of course, our shared commitment to improving the mental health and well-being of others, of enabling others to help themselves, of somehow meeting a need which is complex, long-standing and possibly hard to contain. It goes without saying, I hope, that I have a natural respect for my clients, an unconditional regard for their individual concerns and personhood;

but, despite all this, as an employee of a secular organization, there is no specific demand on me to act as a witness to the life of Christ: no demand except, perhaps, that one I committed myself to last week at the Sunday Eucharist and the Sunday Eucharist before that, but have somehow left behind in the day-to-day trappings of my everyday life.

In his book *Finding Sanctuary: Monastic Steps for Everyday Life,* Christopher Jamison, the Abbot of Worth Abbey, recalls the countless occasions on which he has been asked, 'Why did you become a monk?' His response is this:

> I have offered various answers for various contexts. But the answer I really wanted to give is: 'I don't know.' I do not know why I became a monk because the reason I joined is not the reason I stayed. I joined thinking I could save the world being a monk; I stayed because the monastery became a place where I discovered my own need to be saved. Before I could offer sanctuary, I had to find it.' (2006, p. 5)

Is this why, I wonder, I am struggling with the nature of Gavin's response about the task of a parish church? Because something in it highlights my own shortcomings, my own failure to respond to the Eucharist in a meaningful way, to carry out its purpose and transformation into the pattern of my own life? 'Before I could offer sanctuary, I had to find it.' The words hit an untold chord. How do we, whether as individuals or as a community of faith, offer sanctuary to others when our own internal bickerings and personal weaknesses fall short of the task before us: that is, to be disciples of Christ?

These questions return me once more to the Eucharist itself. Again I am loath to admit that the strength of the Eucharist – its capacity to absorb, heal and transform – has somehow not fully registered with me for the first three-and-something decades of my life. It was only at a recent 'quiet day' at our local convent that I started to have a glimpse of how much I have missed. The 'quiet day' was sanctuary indeed. I whiled away several hours in one of the convent's rooms, reading little, sitting a great deal, and just enjoying the silence the day offered me. Towards the beginning of it I spent an hour with one of the sisters, and during this hour I told her of a personal situation which has been troubling me for some years. I struggled to articulate it, to maintain my own need for composure as I poured out in rambling form my grief and sense of loss.

When I had finished, I looked to the sister for her response. For half my life, it seems, I have somehow been taken up with words and language, be this through literature or psychology, and now as I sat in one of the convent's rooms I realized I was once again looking for something tangible – something verbal, intellectual even, on which I could hook my pain and start to understand it. But the sister's response was not as I expected. She spoke gently and with confidence about the power of the Eucharist, of how much it can heal and transform our lives simply by taking our troubles and concerns to the Eucharist itself. She said she would take my own situation to the Eucharist each day. I knew she would and, through her spirit of generosity and deep-rooted faith, I felt as though I was able to take my first step towards my own inner sanctuary.

*   *   *

If, in my own life, my inner sanctuary is at best fragile and hard to locate, what happens in a parish community when a terrible trauma takes place and an entire body of people is affected? When a priest's ministry is cut short suddenly, the sanctuary of a church is threatened, even overturned, with traumatic and immediate effect. By the same token the stability of each individual's inner world is also threatened. Caroline Garland describes the effect of a trauma on any 'Given Group' in her essay 'The Traumatised Group' as follows:

> All Given Groups function around a primary task. It is that bit of work which has to be carried out successfully if the existence of the group itself is to continue, its raison d'être . . . When the members of a Given Group suffer a traumatic event, everything changes suddenly and without warning. Quite suddenly, the primary task has vanished, and another far more immediate task has replaced it – that of survival . . . It might take years for any institution to recover from such an event, and certainly it would be much changed by what had happened. (1998c, pp. 188–9)

While the notion of survival did not have literal value for the parishioners of Fulham Fields – their own lives were not themselves endangered – the threat on the sanctuary of their community was very real indeed.

On the Sunday following David's death, the area bishop celebrated the Eucharist at St Andrew's. Amid the aftermath of trauma and the grief, the sacramental rite must have held unique meaning indeed. When Gavin and I arrived some 18 months later, I found that to remember the parish's recent history during the eucharistic prayer somehow gave voice, quite unintentionally, to my own, often unspoken stories of loss and disintegration. What is it that calls us to witness and partake in a place of brokenness? A call to heal? A call to learn from that place's own ability to heal and be healed? Or is it the voice of our brokenness and internal devastation, seeking sanctuary that we might provide it? I do not know. But Gavin and I did feel called to St Andrew's and it seems testimony to the Christian story that, when everyday words and comprehension fail us, the strength of the Eucharist is an intervention in itself.

Mental health and the Eucharist

When, at a priest's licensing, he is asked, 'Will you care for the people of this parish in the name of Christ?' (Kuhrt, 1997) he is above all being asked to be, not to do. This task of being is a challenge for each and every one of us. In his book *On Becoming a Person: A Therapist's View of Psychotherapy* (1967), Carl Rogers sets about defining the characteristics of what he terms any 'helping relationship'. The term refers to 'a relationship in which at least one of the parties has the intent of promoting the growth, development, maturity, improved functioning, improved coping with life of the other. The other, in this sense, may be one individual or group' (p. 39). Rogers does not present a didactic version of these defining characteristics but rather invites his reader to engage in a series of questions and considerations, the first four of which seem to have particular relevance here:

1.   Can I *be* in some way which will be perceived by the other person as trustworthy, as dependable or consistent in some deep sense?
2.   Can I be expressive enough as a person that what I am will be communicated unambiguously?
3.   Can I let myself experience positive attitudes toward this other person – attitudes of warmth, caring, liking, interest, respect?
4.   Can I be strong enough as a person to be separate from the other? Can I be a sturdy respecter of my own feelings, my own needs, as

well as his? Can I own and, if need be, express my own feelings as something belonging to me and separate from his feelings? Am I strong enough in my own separateness that I will not be downcast by his depression, frightened by his fear, nor enough engulfed by his dependency? . . . When I can freely feel this strength of being a separate person . . . I am not fearful of losing myself. (pp. 50–2)

These questions resonate strongly not only with Gavin's relationship with individual parishioners but also with his relationship with the St Andrew's community as a whole. In order for a priest's relationship with his flock to be truly respectful, he needs to be honest with himself about the mixed feelings it generates in him: feelings of frustration as well as feelings of empathy, warmth and regard.

Carl Rogers describes how, from a humanistic perspective, the process of unconditional regard and acceptance can be both difficult and painful. From a Christian faith perspective, the challenges of this bring us full circle to the Eucharist once more and its sacramental capacity for transformation. The process emphasizes not specific theories or inter-ventions – though of course these have their place too – but rather the wonder of the eucharistic feast, in which a priest is allowed to be and God's grace is allowed to do its work.

Integrating Mind and Spirit (Part 5)

Transformations

The sacrament of the Eucharist communicates the extent of God's care and concern for his people – understanding failure, offering hospitality, dispensing healing and transforming lives as a result. As disciples of Christ we are called to grapple with this divine benchmark of brokenness and healing, of human breakdown and God's grace. Just as paradox underpins the mystery of salvation, so too we are asked to recognize the same elements of mystery alive in those who are present to pain and suffering. The challenge of doing this in a way that is real, that does not in any way underestimate or trivialize the suffering of people with mental health problems (and those around them) is great. How, therefore, can we hope to mirror the Eucharist's core traits of disturbance and integration? And in what ways can it ground us in serving others?

Practical implications

- In any pastoral encounter with somebody with mental health difficulties, the role of the priest is to seek to offer some degree of containment to the person in need. To be a 'container' for others' anxieties, we need to have structures in place so that our own anxieties can also be contained.[1] For the priest, this may be found at a variety of levels: in the Eucharist itself, in priestly colleagues or more specifically in a spiritual director. The need for more specialist supervision, often overlooked, may also be considered.

• It is easy to forget the power of the Eucharist. Just as psychology can offer no quick fixes, neither of course can the Eucharist. But inviting an individual to attend this service, offering a reminder that it is there to be celebrated again and again in the same place at the same time(s) each week, offers an immediate opportunity for containment and possible healing.

• By recognizing the complexity of mental health issues, we recognize our own limitations. This highlights the need to access other areas of support for an individual (e.g. friends, family) as well as seek referral to other agencies, i.e. health (e.g. GP, psychiatrist, community psychiatric nurse), social services and education (if applicable) and voluntary agencies (e.g. MIND). Entering into dialogue with other family members or outside agencies can help ensure that the nature of support being given is complimentary. That said, the process needs to be done sensitively and collaboratively, respecting an individual's confidentiality (only broken if concerned about their own or another's safety).

• It may be appropriate to access or develop support structures within the church which respond to the individual's needs and the place they are at: for example, pastoral visiting, prayer groups, lunchtime clubs, visits to the theatre and so on.

Questions for individual reflection and/or discussion

1. In what ways are mental health needs being addressed in your church? How might people with mental health needs be further supported?

2. If the sacrament of the Eucharist offers healing, how might your church more fully realize this?

3. How might your church seek to balance an increased need for 'success' (viability and accountability) with an appropriate awareness of or response to mental health and disturbance in the parish?

4. What do you feel God is asking of you and of your church? What is its particular giftedness?

A prayer of thanksgiving

Holy Trinity of God,
in Communion you offer your children new possibilities.
You share our deepest needs,
in you we find the source of our being.
You invite us to the table of fellowship,
and we dance to the song of creation.
We thank you for your transforming love,
that we might realize our vocation in you.
Amen.

Part 6

Moving On

In these final two chapters, as we reach the journey's end we look back in order to look forward. From a liturgical perspective, the process is rooted in the last movement of the liturgy, the Dismissal, in which the people are commissioned to live the life of Christ in the world. From a psychological perspective, this final stage is about evaluating the therapeutic process. Ideally this helps bring about 'a good ending', one that enables an individual to plan for his or her future and cope more readily with the challenges that the world presents.

Chapter 11

The Dismissal

I had decided to leave St Andrew's. The decision was not made unilaterally. Various interests were at stake, not least the parish. What would become of its people? My leaving would determine another interregnum only three years after the ending of the previous one. Clearly I wanted the parish to continue its journey of healing and growth. I was fearful that my leaving would create further trauma among the people that I had come to love.

I was fortunate to have at my disposal an adviser sponsored by the diocese who gave me permission to think through the complexity of issues involved. I struggled to voice my real feelings: my concern that I would be abandoning the people whom I cared for and wanted to protect, while at the same time suffering from exhaustion and a failing belief that I could sustain my ministry there. It became clear that I had a choice: either to stay at St Andrew's for the longer term, prepared to adopt a slower pace, or to leave now. During these discussions, which lasted some months, various difficult questions emerged: not least, was I unwittingly contributing to the inertia and apathy in the parish which I had worked so hard to counter? This was a painful process, but I started to sense the possibility that I was being led out of the parish. I hoped I had at least started what God had asked me to do – namely, to be a healing presence in the community – and I wondered whether I was now being called to new pastures. I therefore set about preparing an ending to my ministry at St Andrew's.

*   *   *

The Dismissal is by far the shortest of the liturgical movements in the drama of the Eucharist. It is the shortest, but it holds much symbolic meaning not only in liturgical terms but also in terms of our life's pilgrimage too. This is the ending of the gathering of the people: the community is dismissed from one sacred space, the church, into another, the world. During my last Eucharist at St Andrew's, the meaning was extended. I was to mark the ending of my ministry to the people, which would bring with it another interregnum. I had conveyed the news to the parish about my decision to leave and had written a pastoral letter in Lent 2005 to try to explain why Jo and I had made such a decision. Although this letter did not explicitly cite all the reasons, it did attempt to communicate something of the truth:

Dear Friends,

The last time I wrote such a letter was before my licensing. I wanted to assure you all then of my prayers at the anniversary of Father David's death. I wrote at a time of new possibilities, new beginnings, as you were preparing to welcome a different style of leadership and a different parish priest.

This letter also picks up the theme of transition after my announcement that I would be leaving the parish in July. Jo and I have been humbled by the generosity shown by so many of you to this sudden news. You have all tried to understand the decision. However, I would like to recap on what we have experienced together and how we can further serve Christ in this parish of Fulham Fields.

In my short time with you (which will be approaching three years this summer) I have been concerned that the church of St Andrew's, Fulham Fields, be allowed to grieve for the loss of Father David, and that healing be applied to the parish where needed. It is for that reason that Jo and I, deliberately but hesitantly, agreed to live in the vicarage. By our living there we hoped that we might encourage the healing process. Many of the memories, hurts and failures within the family of the church have been, or are on the way to being, healed. But there is much reconciling work still to be done among our church family.

Much of the substance of my teaching and preaching has
focused on discipleship and calling – the sheer thrill and excite-
ment of being made in the image of God to share his likeness.
What this means is that we are all loved by God without exception. I believe St Andrew's is a very special community of faith
which offers many signs of God's kingdom, particularly within
the nature of our composition. Not many churches have such a
diverse mixture of people worshipping alongside each other. This
is a gift which marks St Andrew's as special, something that I will
always remember.

I believe that God calls us to the places of need and hope. It is
within our own need and hope that we should all be praying for a
new priest to encourage the work that God has given this community to do. Pray, then, for a person who will lead you to the
places where God wants his pilgrim people to be. Please do not
rely on a person who will solve all problems. We are disciples,
given authority through our baptism to take ownership of the
Church of Christ, to be co-workers with our Lord. Pray for a
leader who has the energy to make disciples of people, leaders of
those who feel unable to take responsibility at present. From a
mission perspective I believe that it should now be 'our duty and
our joy' to take more responsibility for the sharing of the gospel
message – responsible in caring for one another within the
church, as well as those who have yet to receive the Good News of
Christ.

We have achieved many small victories and we should thank
God for these, including the seasonal approach to our worship,
the new Children's Church, the improvements to the building,
tighter financial controls, to name but a few. I thank all of you for
your prayers and the part that you have played in our time
together. I would, however, ask you to consider continuing to
grapple with this question, 'What more can I do to share Christ's
communion?' This is a big question which challenges our faith
and I hope one that leads us to God's heart.

The priest who will succeed me needs your help, hope and
devotion. The maintenance of the church, for example, should
not be his major consideration. He needs to be freed up to share
the mission of the parish, to encourage, facilitate and empower all

of you to pastor, to teach, to heal, and to evangelize (and, yes, to clean)! It is the role of the priest to engage the flock with the wind of the Spirit of God. It is a poor theological model which expects the priest to do all things for all people – we all need to get involved in the work, the prayer and the fellowship.

With my prayers for you during this time of journey and exploration as we continue to follow Christ in the wilderness.

In communion,

Gavin

My letter addressed many of the different issues that I had faced, but also looked to the future of the parish with great hope. Nonetheless many misgivings remained: Was I being honest to God in deciding to leave? Was this my selfish voice or God's vocational pull? Many of these questions would remain unanswered; such is the discipline of seed-sowing which is the nature of parish ministry.

The mystery of the Christ-life, the wonder of the incarnation today is that God finds a dwelling place in us. We are the hosts of God. This thought is a counterbalance to those who feel stigmatized by their mental health. Those sufferers of a disturbance should know that God dwells in them. Living the Christ-life is our ultimate vocation: 'If you continue in my word, you are truly my disciples' (John 8.31). The Eucharist is a missionary rite – it sends us out into the world, commissioning us to live in love and peace, to be Christ's disciples today. This is why, at the end of the eucharistic celebration, I decided to give the blessing from the St Andrew's Road door of the church, asking the congregation to turn from facing the altar, to the door. I wanted to reinforce the theology in a dramatic way that, as the Orthodox Christians believe, the liturgy after the liturgy is about to begin. In other words, all that we have brought, listened to, shared and been gifted in the Eucharist are to be used as missionary tools as we walk into the world outside the church. The congregation is commissioned by the priest to go out into the world to love and serve the Lord. This echoes Jesus' commission to his disciples (Matthew 10.5–14; 28.16–20). Christ's followers seek people to bring them into relationship with God. The Eucharist is a mission-shaped rite.

The often-quoted meaning of the word 'Mass' is that it derives from the Latin verb *missum* meaning 'sent'. The disciples are sent out into the world; they are sent on a mission to reconcile, share and transform the world. Without this missionary perspective, the Eucharist would become a mere religious function serving those whose hearts are turned in upon themselves.

The blessing was God's final word to encapsulate all that had been celebrated and all that will be, reminding me of Dag Hammarskjöld's words that I used during my last Eucharist at St Andrew's: 'For all that has been, thanks; for all that shall be, yes.' The blessing represents the sacred seal of approval for all of the sacramental activity that has taken place in church and that will continue in the nitty-gritty of everyday life. Foster describes the nature of blessing as follows:

> Someone once likened the idea of God's blessing to his smiling at us. The psalmist uses the image in Psalm 67, where he lets his face shine on us. Can we let him look at us and let his face shine on us? Are we ready to learn what his blessing means? Heaven can be found in the Charing Cross Road. (2005, pp. 29–30)

As I stood at the back of the church of St Andrew's, Fulham Fields, as priest to give the Blessing for the very last time, I was surprised to hear that I was the one being blessed. The roles of priest and people had turned full circle. The small choir had gathered around the piano, they had rehearsed Rutter's blessing from Psalm 67, 'The Lord bless you and keep you'. The fragility of their song and the poignancy of the moment moved me to tears. During that short offering of blessing, I felt nothing but love emanating from those whom I had attended to. I could not contain my distress and all the other emotions that were associated with grief, loss and change. My tears represented guilt and concern for this community of people that in my worst moments I felt I had abandoned. Surely, though, this blessing was God's work. The vulnerable, the needy, the resilient, the strong – all became the priest of God for me. God's Spirit was with us.

Chapter 12

Psychological Evaluation

It was my last day at work and I had gone in to clear my desk once and for all. By now I had seen my last family some several days previously and attended any final meetings. All that remained was the administrative task of ensuring that reports were complete and signed, that case notes were up to date, and that referral letters had been sent out where necessary. The task of closing a large caseload is always a difficult one, particularly when, as in my case, there was as yet no appointed successor to fulfil my role. Nonetheless I had known of my departure several months in advance and this had helped me plan, with families and colleagues alike, for a series of endings which I hoped would be as least disruptive as possible. In many cases this had meant fully discharging a client; in some cases, however, I had agreed with the family to refer them on, be this to a different service or, in a few cases, to my supervisor who could continue with the work herself. Where the latter was appropriate, we had met jointly with the family first to try and ensure as smooth a transition as possible. In all cases, though, some form of closure was necessary as my contact was to come to an end.

The very nature of an ending can bring with it a whole host of feelings, and this is true for the therapist and client alike. As psychologists or any 'helping professional', we have a duty to be aware of our own feelings and how these might impact on the therapeutic relationship itself. For clients, an ending might elicit a range of responses: fear, a sense of abandonment or bereavement, ambivalence, sometimes regret. Endings can have a sneaky habit of reawakening, whether consciously or unconsciously, old feelings of loss and disappointment. By the same token, however, endings can go hand in hand with a positive sense that progress has been made. In collaboration with parents and, where appropriate, children also, I would seek to consider the resources they now felt able to draw upon to enable them to manage the complicated, often strenuous task of living with disability. Where mental health was also a factor in a family's story, be this in the child or parent, particular emphasis was placed on considering the structures that individuals now felt they had to hand. Ideally these would incorporate a combination of internal and external structures – an individual's increased resilience, for example, combined with a greater access to other services available.

This process of looking back in order to look forward goes to the heart of psychological evaluation. It is helpful at this point to review an individual's strengths and vulnerabilities, to consider which factors might protect somebody in the future should the same difficulties recur. It is equally helpful to consider those factors that might place an individual or family at risk of relapse – the recurrence, for example, of depression or anxiety, or a pattern of behaviour in one's child which, symptomatic often of wider family issues, feels unmanageable. There are countless standardized measures available that can help validate this evaluation process. By asking a client, for example, to complete a depression or behaviour inventory at the start of therapy, and then at different junctures throughout, it is possible to try and achieve some kind of quantitative measure of what progress has been made. Positive outcomes can also be deduced from concrete steps such as a child's successful transition to a new school or increased independence. These measures and indications help quantify the process of evaluation. They can, however, only ever form part of the picture.

Evaluation is not a finite event that occurs merely at the end of therapy. Ideally it should be an ongoing process which enables a psychologist and client, in collaboration with one another, constantly to review and refine the strengths and limitations of treatment. The potential pitfalls of this process, however, particularly as the end is in sight, need always to be borne in mind. In my clinical capacity, I need to be aware of my own desire to believe that a client is making progress, particularly when I am aware that my departure is imminent and there is no one to take my place. In return, many clients might feel a need to appease their psychologist, as it were, to assure them that the process has indeed been helpful. This process is not necessarily conscious and may of course apply to some cases more than others. The subjective nature of the feelings involved needs, though, to be held keenly in mind when we seek to look back objectively on what has taken place. For this reason, the mixed nature of my feelings informed a key part of my supervision as I prepared for the great number of endings and closures in my last post.

*   *   *

I do not, I confess, like endings. I found it particularly difficult, therefore, that my departure from St Andrew's was, in many ways, untidy. Our last weekend, Sunday Eucharist and celebrations to one side, should have been spent packing. However, complications and delays with our move meant that all packing had been suspended. Keen to leave once we had said our goodbyes, it had been arranged that we would spend the interim period at my parents. The house therefore had a strange quality: neither packed nor unpacked, with no particular ending in sight, it seemed in suspension once more. When we turned the key on the Monday night, I did not know that I would never go back to it; that, when our departure finally came to bear, only Gavin would return to meet with the removals van.

For me, my departure from St Andrew's was a flat moment, a marked contrast to the careful beginning we had planned and worked towards three years previously. The key exception to this was the Sunday Eucharist itself and, strangely enough, relates to a singular and unexpected moment when my personal and professional lives did finally come together. The occasion was during the Peace when I shook hands not with one of the regular congregation (though of course I did this with many) but with the mother of the first child, Sara, I had seen in my post at the child development service. It had not been an 'easy' case in the first stages. Sara had a diagnosis of autism, and her mother, who was struggling to bring her up alone, saw little to no value in my role. As the relationship progressed, these feelings changed and a relationship of mutual trust was established. It had been over two years since I had seen Sara's mother. Nonetheless, as I sighted her in the pews I needed little reminder of her and Sara's story and, before I had time to consider my actions, I crossed over to shake hands. I felt sure Sara's mother had seen me too. I went over, not out of courtesy or goodwill but from a strong impulse that had taken me unawares. At a crossroads in my life when I was struggling with Gavin's and my decision to leave, my own sense of loss and vulnerability was strangely present in that meeting. I was struck by a need on both our parts to shake hands and say those words aloud, 'Peace be with you'; not to place a value on the 'work' that we had achieved together but on the relationship that remained, one whose purpose would be unspoken and unseen in that context but which, for me at least, would offer some small, unquantifiable comfort in my departing.

The meeting had many echoes of that tension in the evaluation process which inevitably exists between those outcomes that can be objectively measured and those outcomes which might never be measured – which are unseen, unspoken, or perhaps just unconscious. To return again for a moment to my clinical work. I might in one session feel that I am alert to a client's needs: I have understood the nature of their difficulties and am able to be curious in a meaningful way about their individual story. Who am I, though, to determine the impact of what I am saying or how I am saying it on the clients themselves? I have sometimes come to the end of a session with a client, felt that it has gone well, arranged the next session, and then never seen him or her again despite any efforts at renewing contact. Equally, I have found myself despondent at the end of a session, struggling to see a way forward and frustrated both by my own and my client's 'stuckness'. In these instances I have sometimes been surprised by unsolicited feedback the following week. The client has gone away, remembered a part of our conversation which has affected her, and in turn found a way of helping herself.

The idiosyncratic, at times unwieldy nature of a clinical psychologist's work bears many resemblances, it seems, to that of parish ministry. For any health practitioner in the NHS, service evaluation, waiting-list targets and 'agenda for change' are all buzz-phrases, to name but three. So too the Church is more and more developing a management model where all parishes are accountable to the diocese. The need for and benefits of this at one level should not be overlooked. In Gavin's own ministry at St Andrew's, as summarized in his closing letter to the parish, a range of interventions helped increase St Andrew's viability and accountability. These 'small victories' were visible and have already been quantified in part: for example, an increase in children's ministry, the improvements to the building and surrounding path, not to mention finances.

How, though, do we begin to evaluate the process of healing which Gavin and I hoped had informed a key part of our short time there?

How, furthermore, do we evaluate the primary task of a parish church 'to make disciples of Christ'? The tension here between a management style of evaluation and God's work is marked. For me, the tension is all the more when we stop to consider the different nature of parishes and their contrasting make-ups. How do we compare, for example, the strengths and viability of one parish which is largely middle-class, high achieving and affluent, with another parish which is of mixed distribution, humbler and poorer? In the field of psychological research, these differences in demographics would be 'factored into' the statistical analysis in an attempt to control for variability. If, to psychologists, these analyses can seem at times a distraction from the primary task and best left to researchers, how does the Church itself begin to grapple with the tension that lies between this kind of expertise and what God is calling it to do?

As Gavin prepared to leave the parish of Fulham Fields, he sought not only to look back and 'evaluate' what had been, but also to pave the way for the parish's journey ahead; to think of its strengths and vulnerabilities, of its characteristics which might nurture its development in the future but which also might place it at risk. Of its unique strengths he referred to St Andrew's as 'a very special community of faith' whose 'diverse mixture of people worshipping alongside one another' marked a particular sign of God's kingdom. He also called on his congregation to consider, 'What more can I do to share Christ's communion?' The question is unique for each and every one of us, and our response will vary throughout the pattern of our lives. Whatever that response, though, I do believe that our own individual mental health in the broadest sense – that is, our 'emotional and spiritual resilience, which enables us to enjoy life and survive pain, disappointment and sadness' (*Promoting Mental Health*, p. 29) is central here not only to ourselves but to the health of the church we call our home. By placing value on this centrality, we are helped, I hope, to acknowledge the fragile centre of our own lives which – at times alive and burgeoning, at others desert-like and barren – is, through our relationship with God, forever sacred and transforming.

*   *   *

When I look back at Gavin's and my time at St Andrew's, even a cursory attempt to quantify our lives there is meaningless and leaves me cold. Who am I to know, to understand, to begin to define what one person's, one people's ministry, might mean to another, not simply over a course of three years but in that tapestry of non-identifiable moments about which we will never know? I for my part did not begin to understand the impact of the St Andrew's people on my own life and journey until we had left them, and the writing of this book has taken me unexpectedly deeper into that process of exploration. But still I know only a little of the individuals, their stories and their meaning which make up the community of Fulham Fields as a whole. I can therefore only speak for myself. For me, my time there was unforeseen, unpredictable and at times painful. It carried me through a journey of brokenness and healing; a journey I am starting to conceive is the journey of the Eucharist itself, and one that underpins the pattern of our lives.

When I embarked on writing this final chapter, I did so with little zeal. Despite the beauty of that final service and the people who made it possible, I approached these final lines with that same sense of loss and anti-climax that I felt when I turned the key on St Andrew's vicarage for the last time. Yet a small bit of me finds space for some contrary voice, and I find I am brought up short about my own feelings of dissatisfaction and loose endings when I return to the final phase of the liturgy itself, the Dismissal. It reminds me of our call at the end not to linger, not to dwell on what has been but to rise and be sent out as disciples of Christ, to get on with his work. As Cassidy writes:

> . . . the rhythm of the Eucharist takes us somewhere else . . . The end is but a beginning . . . But we do resist it, don't we? Isn't it funny that, all over the world, after communion, after the commissioning that occurs with the blessing, all Anglicans kneel down again? It is as though we were trying to hang on to that intimacy. It would be a bit like those women in Matthew's gospel, after being sent out to Jesus, saying to Jesus, 'Hang on, hang on, we'll go when we're ready. We just want to wait a while and savour the moment.' (2001, pp. 110–11)

Sometimes I look back and I imagine that I was not quite ready to leave my life at St Andrew's; that I had not fully appreciated what we had until we left it; that I did not say my goodbyes quite as I would have wished. But now, as I look forward and prepare to finish writing, I think perhaps it does not matter whether I was 'ready' after all. My strengths, my vulnerabilities, the unseen threads of my own internal world, all this had been absorbed and transformed by the Eucharist and would be so again. I had been sent out from Fulham Fields one final time and, though I did not know it at the time, I had responded, at least in part, to the urgency of the dismissal.

Integrating Mind and Spirit (Part 6)

Moving on

An individual's story of mental health difficulties may refer to a single period in time, a one-off episode triggered by specific circumstances, hopefully never to be repeated. Or those difficulties may be cyclical in nature, encountering times of breakdown and crisis as well as times of rehabilitation and recovery. For some, debilitating mental health may be experienced as a small death, of dying to the world and loving relationships within it. During these periods the carer needs particular support, not knowing whether the episode will lead to renewed health or continued pain.

For the parish priest, the Dismissal represents a time of uncertainty also. From the containment and safety of the Eucharist, participants venture out into places of risk and vulnerability. Yet the question of faith necessitates handing over the responsibility of care to God. In both the context of the Dismissal and the recovery stage of a mental health crisis, the priest and carer are asked to have confidence to give the person or people to God – a leap of faith which may go hand in hand with 'letting go'.

This 'letting go' is a key requisite for pastoral work and does not mean absolving care or responsibility. It is important to recognize that trust can be difficult both to establish and to maintain when mental health is fragile. At the same time, where this trust is present, it is possible for that relationship of trust to continue long after separation takes place. A truly theological mark of this trust will continue through the bond or covenant that comes through holding the 'cared-for' in mind – what Christians call prayer.

Practical implications

A priest is called throughout the course of his ministry to seek to enable others. This process of enablement can be at times challenging, at times hard to quantify; it may even go unnoticed – it can also be deeply rewarding. This process does not, alas, come armed with a toolkit, a neat little package of 'do's' and 'don'ts' for mental health. How might, then, a priest look back and consider: 'Did I do that right? What would I do next time? How will they be when I am not there? How will *I* be when I am not there ...?'

For a priest to grapple with these questions, it may be of benefit:

* To help both the individual concerned and/or carer to understand the strengths and resources they have developed. This will help strengthen an individual's mental health resilience.
* To help both the individual concerned and/or carer to understand areas of vulnerability, including possible triggers and stress points. This can increase an individual's and/or carer's insight into the mental health issues. It can also help an individual/carer to recognize warning signs in the future so they are better able to help themselves or seek help sooner.
* To try to identify the strengths and vulnerabilities of the church community as a whole. This will better enable individuals within the community to help not only themselves and others, but also the life of the church, particularly at times of fragility or transition.

And finally:

* To continue to evaluate one's ministry and the pastoral encounters within it . . . in other words, to reflect theologically on one's discipleship, to seek to learn from past mistakes and to try to find out where God is in all of this.

Questions for individual reflection and/or discussion

1. In what ways does your church encourage you to go out and care for others?
2. What key challenges have you faced as a church community recently? How have you addressed these? What strengths and vulnerabilities have these challenges highlighted?
3. Reflect on ways in which you now feel more able to respond to issues of mental health and healing in your church community.
4. With the benefit of theological reflection, in what ways have mental health issues influenced your ministry?

A prayer of blessing

May the God of Welcome call us into his fellowship of love.
The God of Incarnation renew the gospel flame in us.
The God of Communion heal our broken soul.
The God of Blessing anoint us with courage and truth.
And the Creator Father,
Redeemer Son,
Sustainer Spirit,
Fill us with heavenly peace now and for evermore.
Amen.

Epilogue

This book will only be meaningful if it strikes a chord in the heart of the human condition called the soul. Setting out to plan this project, we had both intended, naively perhaps, to attempt to put mental health on the church map by writing a more formal, didactic account. This proved in practice less than satisfactory and ultimately unauthentic. We revised our original plan and started to write freely, without limitations, remembering much of our past experiences and encountering both joy and pain. The project became a book of surprises. The more that we wrote, the more we journeyed into our personal stories. It was never our intention to grapple so intensely with our own demons, yet how could we describe the life of the parish of St Andrew's, Fulham Fields, without engaging with our own vulnerabilities too? The process of story-telling within the two disciplines of theology and psychology became for us a valuable encounter.

But at the core of this book are the questions which flow from the undeniable reality that mental health is a key aspect of the life of any parish today. We have tried to explore some of the vulnerabilities of both laity and clergy, and have placed these in the specific context of a parish where trauma and healing are central to its narrative. We have not given – cannot give – any definitive answers to the fragility which arises from the disturbance of mind and spirit. We have, though, tried to illustrate some key issues which may be of benefit to the church community. We hope to have ventured upon another task of seed sowing, attempting to bring to light an area of life that is often shrouded by myth and stigma.

For my part, reflecting upon the liturgy of the Eucharist was a natural response to my own experience of depression. The liturgy contained order, stability and, above all, hope that life was to continue. The liturgy proclaims the good news that Christ triumphs over death and, in triumphing over death, Jesus overcomes also all disturbances of mind and spirit. The liturgy encourages us to understand that this work of Christ continues today in the unknown, unseen, even unspeakable places of our internal worlds. And so I would like to return to the frontispiece in which Jo introduced a description of the encounter with our human condition. Maybe it is apt to reposition these words at the end of the book, and at the end of this particular journey:

There is a place within each of our sacred selves that very few would willingly visit, and yet this place is probably more frequented than any other we know. It is a fragile place, fused with the mind and the spirit. It has many terrains, many voices and many magnitudes. So well hidden is this place that, when we find ourselves on its threshold, we turn our gaze from its path and, deep within our unconscious self, a voice is spoken: I am not here, I have not visited this place, tell no one. And so in that moment of buried recognition, we re-frame what we have encountered and seek to sanitize what we have known.

Or do we? Perhaps instead we open the door and risk entering a place from which we might never return; from a place that is so riddled with stigma and myth that, steeped in our society though it is, it only forms the subject of discourse in specialist circles or with a trusted few. It is a sensitive place and it must not be spoken of too loudly. Its limits are poorly defined and its nature unpredictable. Unique to each and every one of us, this place is, we suggest, the landscape of our mental health.

We have spent time in confession, we have been reconciled to God, shared our most intimate stories, wondered at the revelation of God before and within us, and have been blessed as holy people to continue as disciples of Christ. I pray that we might sense the sacredness of our souls and the beauty of God's purpose for us. I especially make this prayer for the people of St Andrew's, Fulham Fields.

GRK

Notes

Introduction

1   *Promoting Mental Health* was produced in conjunction with both the NHS (the National Institute for Mental Health in England) and the charity 'Mentality', which promotes mental health. The document was designed as a tool that can be used flexibly within parishes, with the specific purpose of generating debate on mental health issues. It is a detailed and practical resource which includes sections on planning and delivering training, and specific activity and workshop session outlines.

2   Information about and citations relating to this conference were obtained from the BBC website: http://news.bbc.co.uk/1/hi/health/321622.stm

3   Source: *Western Mail*, Friday 14 March 2008.

4   Nick Tolson in his essay 'Clergy Lifestyle Theory' cites six generic reasons for violence against clergy, and discusses some of the complexities of making sense of these. Cited causes are: alcohol, drugs (either 'high' or in need of drugs), mental illness, anger, fear or medical illness.
    See: http://www.nationalchurchwatch.com/the_clergy_lifestyle_theory.pdf

Chapter 1

1   The title of this book was inspired by a school chaplains' conference held by the Bloxham Project in April 2005, entitled 'Disturbed by the Spirit: Discipleship and Change'.

2   L'Arche is an international organization of communities for adults with developmental disabilities which fosters inclusion and belonging – see http://www.larche.org.uk. Originally founded by Jean Vanier in France in 1964, its communities are now worldwide. Nouwen died while living with the Toronto community in Canada in 1996.

Chapter 3

1   See David Stancliffe, *God's Pattern: Shaping Our Worship, Ministry and Life* (2003), London: SPCK.

2   *The Oxford Dictionary of the Christian Church*, ed. F. L. Cross and E. A. Livingstone (1997), Oxford: Oxford University Press, p. 988.

3   All Bible references are taken from the New Revised Standard Version (1989), Oxford: Oxford University Press.
4   Brother Roger of Taizé frequently used this gospel imperative to inspire young people in their searching for a relationship of trust with God.
5   This is the mystery of faith that is proclaimed by the priest and the people echoing St Paul's first letter to the community at Corinth: 1 Corinthians 11.26; 1 Corinthians 15.19-24.

Chapter 5
1   All *Common Worship* material cited in this book is taken from the 2000–6 edition.
2   From a prayer by the seventeenth-century Bishop of Geneva, Francis de Sales. Unfortunately, no original citation for this prayer has been found.

Chapter 9
1   These criteria included the following: energized by faith; outward-looking focus; seeks to find out what God wants; faces the cost of change and growth; builds community; makes room for others; does a few things and does them well.
2   This phrase is taken from the title of Arundhati Roy's book, *The God of Small Things* (1997), London: HarperCollins, as well as being a popular theological idiom.
3   Source: Eucharistic Prayer, *Common Worship*.

Integrating Mind and Spirit (Part 5)
1   Containment is a psychoanalytic concept, deriving from Bion. It 'describes the process of processing anxiety and emotions so that the ability to think is restored. One practical aspect of this [in parent–child work] is that the professional actively listens and puts the story together with the parent, before attempting to give any advice or behaviour management'. Cited from: http://www.solihull.nhs.uk/solihullapproach/about.asp

Bibliography

Archbishops' Council (2000) *A Time to Heal: The Development of Good Practice in the Healing Ministry: A Handbook*. London: Church House Publishing.

Axline, V. M. (1964) *Dibs: In Search of Self*. London: Penguin Books.

Berryman, J. W. (2002) *The Complete Guide to Godly Play, Volume 2*. Denver, Colorado: Living the Good News.

Bion, W. R. (1961) *Experiences in Groups, and other Papers*. London: Tavistock, cited by C. Garland (1998) 'The Traumatised Group', *Understanding Trauma: A Psychoanalytical Approach* (ed. C. Garland). London: Duckworth.

Burnham, A. (2001) *A Manual of Anglo-Catholic Devotion*. Norwich: Canterbury Press.

CARIS (Christian Action and Response in Society), London Diocesan Board for Social Responsibility (1996) 'Knocking at Heaven's Door: Challenges and Opportunities Presented by the Casual Caller in the Parish'. http://www.london.anglican.org/Organisation/Regulations/Safety/Knocking%20at%20Heaven's%20Door%20Full%20Report.doc

Carr, A. and McNulty, M. (eds) (2006) *The Handbook of Adult Clinical Psychology: An Evidence Based Practice Approach*. London: Routledge.

Carson, M. L. S. (2008) *The Pastoral Care of People with Mental Health Problems*. London: SPCK.

Cassidy, J. P. (2001) 'The Post Communion Prayer – Living Sacrifice', *Living the Eucharist: Affirming Catholicism and the Liturgy* (ed. S. Conway). London: Darton, Longman and Todd.

Celebrating Common Prayer (1992) SSF Sunday Morning Prayer.

Chrysostomos, A. (trans. 1980) *The Ancient Fathers of the Desert*. Hellenic College Press: Brookline.

Common Worship 2000–6, Archbishops' Council of the Church of England. Church House Publishing.

Cottrell, S. (2001) 'The Gathering Rite', *Living the Eucharist: Affirming Catholicism and the Liturgy* (ed. S. Conway). London: Darton, Longman and Todd.

Countryman, L. W. (2001) 'The Liturgy of the Word', *Living the Eucharist: Affirming Catholicism and the Liturgy* (ed. S. Conway). London: Darton, Longman and Todd.

Dallos, R. and Draper, R. (2005) *An Introduction to Family Therapy: Systemic Therapy and Practice.* 2nd Edition. Maidenhead: Open University Press.

de Waal, E. (2003) *Lost in Wonder: Rediscovering the Spiritual Art of Attentiveness.* Norwich: Canterbury Press.

—— (2006) 'A Wonder-Filled Life', *On-Line Catholics: An Independent Australian e-journal.* Issue 87, 18 January 2006. http://www.onlinecatholics.acu.edu.au/ issue87/commessay1.html

Ehlers, A. and Clark, D. M. (2000) 'A Cognitive Model of Posttraumatic Stress Disorder', *Behaviour Research Therapy,* 38.4, pp. 319–45.

Engel, G. E. (1977) 'The Need for a New Medical Model', *Science,* 1996, pp. 129–36.

Forest, J. (2002) *Confession: Doorway to Forgiveness.* New York: Orbis Books.

Foster, D. (2005) *Reading with God: Lectio Divina.* London: Continuum.

Freud, S. (1920) 'Beyond the Pleasure Principle', Standard Edition, 15, 1–64, cited by C. Garland (1998) 'Thinking about Trauma', *Understanding Trauma: A Psychoanalytical Approach* (ed. C. Garland). London: Duckworth.

Garland, C. (1998a) 'Introduction: Why Psychoanalysis?', *Understanding Trauma: A Psychoanalytical Approach* (ed. C. Garland). London: Duckworth.

—— (1998b) 'Thinking about Trauma', *Understanding Trauma: A Psychoanalytical Approach* (ed. C. Garland). London: Duckworth.

—— (1998c) 'The Traumatised Group', *Understanding Trauma: A Psychoanalytical Approach* (ed. C. Garland). London: Duckworth.

Gilbert, P. (2002) 'Understanding the Biopsychosocial Approach: Conceptualization', *Clinical Psychology,* 14, pp. 13–17.

Holy Bible: New Revised Standard Version (NRSV), (1989) Oxford: Oxford University Press.

Jamison, C. (2006) *Finding Sanctuary: Monastic Steps for Everyday Life.* London: Orion.

Kiesler, D. J. (1999) *Beyond the Disease Model of Mental Disorders.* New York: Praeger.

King , N. (trans. 2004) *The New Testament.* Suffolk: Kevin Mayhew.

Kirk, J. (1989, 1998) 'Cognitive–Behavioural Assessment', in: *Cognitive Behaviour Therapy for Psychiatric Problems: A Practical Guide,* eds K. Hawton, P. M. Salkovskis, J. Kirk and D. M. Clark. Oxford: Oxford University Press.

Kuhrt, G. (1997) 'Clergy Security: A Discussion Paper'. Advisory Board: Church of England.

Lindsay, S. J. E. and Powell, G. E. (1994) 'Practical Issues of Investigation in Clinical Psychology', in: *Clinical Adult Psychology,* 2nd Edition, eds S. J. E. Lindsay and G. E. Powell. London: Routledge.

Milner-White, E. (1966) *A Procession of Passion Prayers.* London: SPCK, cited in *A Manual of Anglo-Catholic Devotion* (2001) ed. Andrew Burnham. Norwich: Canterbury Press.

Moltmann, J. (1967) *Theology of Hope.* London: SCM Press.

National Churchwatch (2007) 'Personal Safety Advice Factsheet'. http://www. ecclesiastical.com/uploads/Personal%20Safety%20Advice%20Factsheet_tcm 9-4544.pdf

Nouwen, H. (1994a) *The Wounded Healer: Ministry in Contemporary Society.* London: Darton, Longman and Todd.

—— (1994b) *The Return of the Prodigal Son: A Story of Homecoming.* London: Darton, Longman and Todd.

Promoting Mental Health: A Resource for Spiritual and Pastoral Care (2004), commissioned by Church of England's Mission and Public Affairs Council and National Institute for Mental Health in England (NIMHE). http://www.cofe. anglican.org/info/socialpublic/homeaffairs/mentalhealth/parishresource.pdf

Rogers, C. R. (1967) *On Becoming a Person: A Therapist's View of Psychotherapy.* Bury St Edmunds, Suffolk: St Edmundsbury Press.

Roth, A. and Fogarty, P. (1996) *What Works for Whom? A Critical Review of Psychotherapy Research.* New York: Guildford Press.

Savage, S. and Watts, F. (2002) 'The Psychology of Church Services', in *Psychology for Christian Ministry* by F. Watts, R. Nye and S. Savage. London: Routledge.

Stancliffe, D. (2003) *God's Pattern: Shaping Our Worship, Ministry and Life.* London: SPCK.

Teasdale, J. D. (1997) 'The Relationship Between Cognition and Emotion: The Mind-in-place in Mood Disorders', *Science and Practice of Cognitive Behaviour Therapy,* eds D. M. Clark and C. G. Fairburn. Oxford: Oxford University Press.

Thorne, B. (2003) *Infinitely Beloved: The Challenge of Divine Intimacy.* London: Darton, Longman and Todd.

Tolson, N. (2007) 'The Clergy Lifestyle Theory: Assessing the Risk of Violence to Clergy'. http://www.nationalchurchwatch.com/the_clergy_lifestyle_theory. pdf.

Walker, A. (1996) *Telling the Story: Gospel, Mission and Culture.* Bristol: The Longdunn Press.

Ward, B. (trans.) (1981) *The Sayings of the Desert Fathers: The Alphabetical Collection.* Oxford: A. R. Mowbray.

Warren, R. and Hodgson, J. (2001) *Growing Healthy Churches: The Archbishops' Initiative for Evangelism.* Springboard.

Watts, F., Nye, R. and Savage, S. (2002) *Psychology for Christian Ministry.* London: Routledge.

Williams, R. (2003) *Silence and Honey Cakes: The Wisdom of the Desert.* Oxford: Lion Books.

—— (2006) Lecture at the School Chaplains' Conference, *Encyclical 80,* autumn 2006.

Young, F. (2001) 'The Great Thanksgiving Prayer', *Living the Eucharist: Affirming Catholicism and the Liturgy* (ed. S. Conway). London: Darton, Longman and Todd.